# Oil Painting

## STEP-BY-STEP

# Oil
# Painting

## STEP-BY-STEP

### By Arthur L. Guptill

Watson-Guptill Publications, New York
Pitman Publishing, London

*To Ernest W. Watson*
*long-time friend, professional colleague*
*and business associate*

*It is a pleasure to offer this word of appreciation*
*to the many friends—both institutions and*
*individuals—who have helped to make this book*
*possible. We are especially indebted to the*
*following for their generous contributions to*
*Part Two: Ernest W. Watson, John Folinsbee,*
*James Penney, Jerry Farnsworth, and Robert Philipp.*

Copyright © 1965 by Watson-Guptill Publications
First published 1965 in New York by Watson-Guptill Publications,
a division of Billboard Publications, Inc.,
One Astor Plaza, New York, N.Y. 10036

Published in England 1974 by Sir Isaac Pitman & Sons Ltd.,
39 Parker Street, Kingsway, London WC2B 5PB
ISBN 0–273-40673–6

Manufactured in the U.S.A.

ISBN 0-8230-3290-6
Library of Congress Catalog Card Number: 65-15945

First Edition, 1953
   Second Printing, 1954
Second Edition, 1958
   Second Printing, 1962
Third Edition, 1965
   Second Printing, 1967
   Third Printing, 1968
   Fourth Printing, 1969
   Fifth Printing, 1971
   Sixth Printing, 1973
   Seventh Printing, 1974

# CONTENTS

# Introduction

EVERYONE CAN LEARN to paint! *You* can learn to paint. I'm not saying that you can become a Titian, a Rembrandt or a Winslow Homer, but if you possess intelligence, an open mind, normal eyesight, a lot of sincere interest plus an equal amount of perseverance, you can acquire the skill—and in a reasonable length of time—to produce very acceptable paintings.

You may be surprised that I say nothing about that much-talked-of thing called talent. I have nothing against talent; in fact I'm all for it. But I have learned after many years of teaching both art students and amateurs by the hundreds that although the talented person may go much farther than the less talented one—or at least can progress more rapidly and with greater ease—anyone, to repeat, no matter how lacking he may seem to be in native "artistic" endowment, can soon be doing competent work provided he has the other qualifications just mentioned. Far more beginners fall by the wayside because of lack of interest, confidence or perseverance than for any other reason.

It may encourage some of you who doubt your own aptitude to know that talented individuals often fail to make full use of their gifts and so are outdistanced by others with less natural capacity. Every art school enrolls many a student who seemingly possesses all of the qualifications for exceptional success but who, as the days and months and years go by, accomplishes disappointingly little, while others who appear to lack almost every requisite but an inexhaustible fund of faith and determination, eventually fight on to win a good share of the highest honors.

Whatever your talents, and regardless of your aims, don't think that any worthwhile accomplishments can be yours unless you are willing—yes, enthusiastic—to work for it. Assuming that your primary interest is in representational painting, in order to get very far you must read books such as this, or take lessons which cover about the same ground. You must learn to observe natural appearances analytically, and you must develop the skill to filter these appearances through your mind as you transfer them to canvas in a suggestive manner and modified form, creating on your flat and limited surface the necessary illusions of size, space, roundness, weight, color, motion, et cetera. Along with your mental exercises, in other words, you must practice, practice, practice, with your paints, simultaneously learning not only to *do* work but also to *evaluate and criticize* what you do with an unprejudiced and discriminating mind.

The rewards of painting are great. I am thinking less of the monetary rewards—for some of you aren't interested in these—than of the deep pleasure and lasting satisfaction which derive from progressing rung by rung up the ladder of achievement. Every day it is your privilege as a painter to set out on an exciting and provocative new adventure, attempting to meet in full at least some part of nature's challenge of line, tone and color. You are not, in short, a mere spectator of something which somebody else is doing, but a participant playing a sort of game by matching your ever-developing skills against nature's complexities of subject matter.

This art of participation is one of the finest things about painting, especially when considered as a pastime. Today in numerous fields too many of us are but spectators, and so we fail to develop or use many of our most vital innate abilities. We *watch* a ball game but do not play. Sitting before our television or radio sets, we *observe* or *listen* to a speech or a musical program. This watching or listening to the other fellow is all right up to a certain point—we can't always be performers—but whatever pleasure or profit it yields reaches us secondhand and can't be compared to the rich recompense which results from getting into an activity ourselves. Let me emphasize this point that too many of us neglect the creative talents with which we were born—most of us have some!—and therefore seldom, if ever, experience the thrill and spiritual uplift which come from such a creative endeavor as working out a musical composition, turning a bit of clay into a ceramic, or producing a picture on a blank sheet of canvas.

So never forget that, as an artist, you are privileged in being not a spectator, but a participant in something very exciting, very stimulating, very rewarding. You are an interpreter of nature's multifarious displays, a magician performing miracles, a creator of canvases which not only bring you pleasure as you paint them—for much of the recompense lies in the mere performance of wielding your brush—but which in their finished form will in all probability continue to satisfy you, and perhaps many others, for a long time to come.

But let me warn you not to expect too much in a hurry. All of this gratifying accomplishment calls for a lot of thinking and doing, so don't expect to advance rapidly or without hard work. I scarcely need to remind you of that trite but true bit of Latin, *ars longa, vita brevis*. For art *is* long and the hours which make up our all-too-short lives have a way of taking wings. But I reiterate that if art is long, it is nevertheless fun—rare fun—and its pursuit can bring you great compensation. But never forget that art *is* a pursuit; you will never quite catch up with it.

This brings us to the sixty-four-dollar question: What can a book like this do for you? A great deal, really, especially if, like thousands of others, you find it necessary to work without a teacher.

Such a book can't, of course, accomplish the impossible. You doubtless know perfectly well that a series of chapters such as these—or more highly specialized books, for that matter, such as we shall recommend from time to time—can only go so far in lessening your period of travail. Neither they, nor any school or teacher, can offer you any open sesame —any short cut to success through six easy lessons. For there is no such short cut. This is not saying that you can't learn a lot from six lessons, or from one. A few words at the right time from the right person can prove priceless. But in the long run much of your knowledge will gradually come to you through personal experimentation and study. Books like this can guide you in this personal effort, however, and that in itself can be of inestimable help. Following such exercises as we offer here, holding your own brush and painting your own pictures, you will take—largely by means of trial and error—your most vital and most gratifying strides.

My stress in the pages to follow will be on representational painting —that type usually referred to as "traditional," "realistic" or "naturalistic." Most of the same principles and practices, however, apply equally well to other types of work with the exception of some extreme "isms."

I shall pass on to you information as to various fundamental technicalities of the *craft* of painting, while discussing certain of the ABC's of painting as an *art*. In addition, I can possibly help you to avoid a number of discouraging and time-consuming pitfalls, while establishing a safe and sane point of view. I shall also try to aid you in sharpening your powers of observation, analysis, retention and invention. If I can teach you to observe comprehendingly, a lot will be accomplished, for then even if your painting effort fails and you ultimately turn from it, your whole life will prove richer for the increased insight which you will have acquired. You will have learned to enjoy and appreciate to a greatly augmented degree many of the esthetic attributes of both art and nature.

As to you amateurs among my readers—and I assume you may be many—never overlook the value of painting as a pastime or hobby. No matter how much you are weighed down with the cares of your daily job or the jumbled mess of world affairs, no matter how distressing your personal problems, nothing can convey you into another world so quickly—a sort of Shangri-la of your very own—as to set up your easel and get under way with your paints. Have you read what Sir Winston Churchill had to say about all this in his delightful and revealing book, *Painting as a Pastime* (Cornerstone)? If not, you should. It's a meaty, wise and witty little volume, drawn from his earlier book, *Amid These Storms* (Scribner's).

In at least one respect you amateurs seem to be far better off, by the way, than the students. For when they ultimately turn professional they will be in danger, heaven forbid, of soon coming to look on their painting as just a routine job, with their main aim one of selling in order to earn a living. For, whatever their present inner inclination, they must some day devote a large part of their time to painting an acceptable, saleable product. But you amateurs can paint what you please, when you please, as you please! You are free.

But to you all, whether amateurs or students, the best of luck! I hope you will get at least a few workable ideas from this book.

ARTHUR L. GUPTILL

# Part One

## HOW TO PAINT IN OILS

# Chapter 1

# THE EQUIPMENT

BEFORE YOU CAN start to paint, you must obviously acquire the necessary canvas, paints and brushes, so, as a prelude to your first "lessons," let's take a look at this essential equipment.

Some beginners make the mistake at the start of buying too many working tools—so many that they feel almost overwhelmed. True, most of us have an accumulative streak, and it *is* fun to splurge on the accoutrements of one's art. But why not spread this pleasure over a longer period, while mastering one item at a time?

Occasionally beginners go to the opposite extreme and waste a tremendous amount of time and effort because of a lack of enough equipment. While an expert can produce a very acceptable painting with but a few things, don't forget that he *is* an expert. I once heard a violin virtuoso play remarkably well on one fiddle string, but it takes me all four to produce a passable result. And quality counts, too. Even *he* couldn't have managed with an inferior instrument any more than you can hope to do your best with low-grade canvases, colors or brushes. On these three particular items there should be little attempt at economy. The beginner who is forced to save can practice his frugality on other things which, though desirable, are comparatively nonessential: for example, a color box, an easel, a sketching stool.

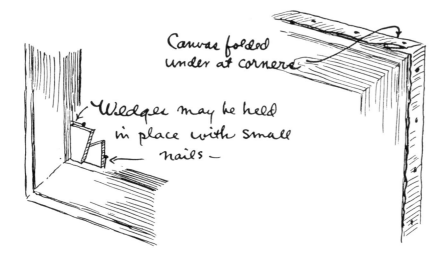

Canvas folded under at corners

Wedges may be held in place with small nails —

STRETCHERS *Canvas is often tacked onto wooden strips which are first interlocked to form a rigid frame. Wedges bring the canvas taut.*

"Unprepared" or "raw" canvas (not made for artists) can also be had. This must be treated in order to prevent the paint from soaking into it. Therefore the novice—like most professionals—will probably select in its place the regular "commercial" or "artists' " canvas—the kind which dealers normally stock. This is ready for use, having previously been "sized" by the manufacturer (often with glue or gelatin and water) and "primed" (generally with white lead—or similar pigment—and oil) to form the painting "ground" on which the artist works. He customarily applies his paints directly to this ground without additional preparation. (See, however, hints on preparing a ground, page 150.)

CANVAS TEXTURES

Canvases possess different textures, some rough, some medium and some smooth, the artist choosing for each painting a texture which he thinks well-adapted to his subject matter, manner of working, size of painting or effect desired. (See Figure 2.) Beginners often like the rougher surfaces, which are encouraging in that anything done on them has in abundance that "oil painting look." Yet the medium or smoother textures are customarily better. They offer less resistance to the brushwork, and are not too conspicuous in finished paintings.

Paintings done on stretched canvas are rather easily damaged. This is no doubt a major reason why artists have been turning more and more to the better types of canvas panels or other forms of rigid supports. Among the latter are Presdwood (Masonite), Vehisote, plywood and illustration board. All but the last of these are building materials. Sometimes the artist glues canvas to such boards; again, he sizes and primes the boards themselves to provide suitable grounds. Ask your dealer to show you what he has in ready-prepared boards.

But this is getting rather too technical, so we shall leave it to the inquisitive reader to turn for fuller information to such books as *The Materials of the Artist* by Max Doerner (Harcourt, Brace & World); *The Artist's Handbook of Materials and Techniques* by Ralph Mayer (Viking); and *Painting Materials and Techniques* by Frederic Taubes (Watson-Guptill). This last book, by the way, is both a useful reference

*Figure 2*

CANVAS  *The selection of canvas depends on such factors as size of painting, subject matter, and personal painting style.*

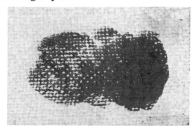

and a comprehensive textbook, going into far greater detail, technically, than we can hope to do in such a general volume as this.

### BRUSHES

There are two common types for oil painting: bristle brushes and sable (or imitation sable) brushes. (See Figures 3 and 4.) Bristle brushes have long been made of hog's hair; some are now said to be of synthetic materials.

*Figure 3*
**BRISTLE BRUSHES** *You will need a fair number of brushes. These show, at actual size, several common types. Use the largest brush you can for every purpose. Keep your brushes clean!*

Of the bristle brushes—the ones most used in oil work—the "brights" are flat, thin brushes with short bristles; the "flats" are thicker with longer bristles. Some of these flat brushes have points which are oval, rather than square. Round brushes with pointed tips—"rounds"—may also be had, but are less generally used. All are rather stiff. (Figure 3.)

Sable brushes, though more frequently employed by the watercolorist, are available for oil painting. They are made both flat and round, common kinds being short hair "brights," pointed "rounds" and flat

20

Round Sable Brush (Pointed)

Round Sable Brush (Flattened Ferrule)

Flat Sable Brush

*Figure 4*
**SABLE BRUSHES** *Though much of your work will be done with the stiffer bristle brushes, sables are useful for some types of painting, especially where fine detail is needed.*

"longs." (Figure 4.) Though springy, they are relatively soft. In oil painting, they are useful for fine detail, for soft brush strokes, and for delicate blendings of colors.

Another type of brush having soft hair is known as a "blender." Often blenders are large and somewhat flat, though they come in a variety of shapes and sizes. (Figure 5.)

Blender (Soft Hair)

*Figure 5*
**BLENDERS** *As a rule, these soft brushes have but occasional use, though much depends on your working methods.*

For varnishing, a flat brush made for the purpose is needed. This can be inexpensive. One inch is a suitable width for all work of modest size. Either your artists' supply dealer or your paint store can furnish it.

A typical selection of painting brushes for the beginner should include a few flat bristles—some with short hairs and some with long—ranging perhaps from No. 2 to No. 8; also, four or five red sables, some round and some flat, starting with No. 3 and running to No. 12 or No. 16. All should preferably have long handles. One or two blenders measuring 1 inch to 1½ or 2 inches would complete the assortment. Gradually, though, you will want to experiment with different brushes until you discover what you like for every need.

Inasmuch as manufacturers do not all use the same numbers for designating brush size, the accompanying illustrations (Figures 3, 4, and 5) reproduce typical brushes at actual size.

It is often well to have several brushes of each common size. Some painters like to have a separate brush at hand for every dominant color in a painting. Others use one brush for light colors and another for dark. Such practices undoubtedly save time and paint, for if but one or two brushes are used throughout they will need very frequent wiping.

### CARE OF BRUSHES

Brushes are rather expensive, so they deserve proper care. Never let paint dry in them. As you work, rinse each brush frequently in some such solvent as turpentine, kerosene or mineral spirits, and then wipe it with a rag. At the close of a painting session, rinse each brush in the solvent even more thoroughly (excess paint can first be squeezed out on newspaper), after which you should wash it painstakingly with warm water (not hot) and laundry soap. Rub the brush on the soap and scrub it with a circular motion on the palm of your hand. Rinse. Then shape—but don't squeeze!—then wet the bristles with the fingers and allow them to dry. *Never stand brushes on their bristles.*

### BRUSH WASHERS

Your dealer can probably furnish you with a brush washer (A, Figure 6), though it is by no means essential. Jerry Farnsworth, in his book *Portrait and Figure Painting* (Watson-Guptill), pictures a somewhat different type

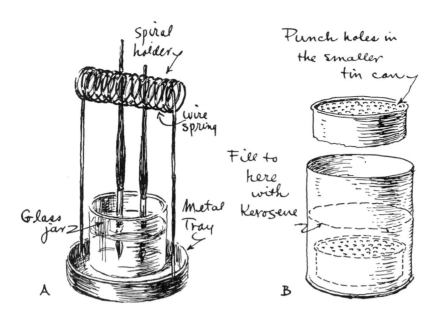

Figure 6

**BRUSH WASHERS** *Manufactured brush washer (A) and Jerry Farnsworth's homemade model (B). Whether or not you have such a gadget, wash your brushes often. Don't let paint dry in them.*

of washer, a simple, homemade affair. (B, Figure 6.) He says: "An excellent brush washer can be made with a medium sized tin can (such as a tomato can) with the top cut out, and a small flat can (tuna fish can) with the bottom cut out. With a hammer and nail, punch holes in the top of the tuna can and slip it inside the larger can. . . . Fill the container halfway with kerosene or mineral spirits, which are the best washing mediums, and you have a very efficient brush washer. . . . The kerosene or mineral spirits will always stay clean because the washed-out paint from your brushes will settle to the bottom of the can. The whole solution should be dumped out occasionally and fresh kerosene added."

**PALETTE AND PAINTING KNIVES**

Such knives are of many kinds. Some are used only (or mainly) for mixing the colors on the palette. Others take the place of brushes—or are used with them—for conveying the paint to the canvas and spreading it in position. The type of knife selected depends on its intended use. For mix-

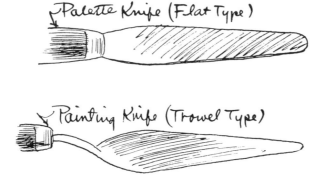

Palette Knife (Flat Type)

Painting Knife (Trowel Type)

*Figure 7*

**PALETTE AND PAINTING KNIVES** *These knives are used not only for mixing paint, but also for applying it. Some painters prefer knives to brushes, at least for much of their work.*

ing paint, a stiff knife—often trowel-shaped—is good. A wide blade aids in this manipulation. For applying paint, the blade can be somewhat more flexible; it is often straight, though preferences in all of these items vary amazingly. Our sketches (Figure 7) show typical selections.

Some artists do all of their painting with knives, using no brushes whatsoever. Knives offer a good starting point as they enable one to paint directly, but most artists turn to brushes for much of their work.

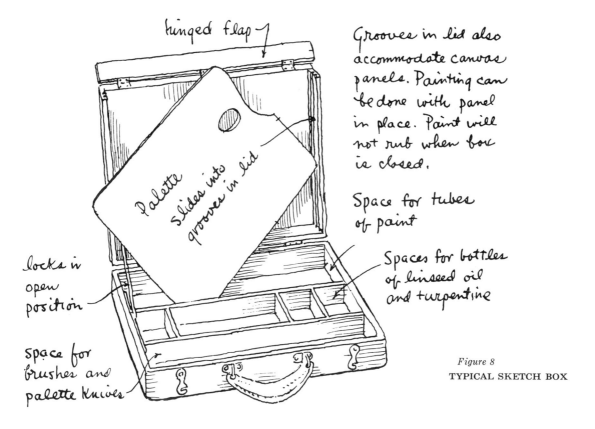

hinged flap

Grooves in lid also accommodate canvas panels. Painting can be done with panel in place. Paint will not rub when box is closed.

Palette slides into grooves in lid

Space for tubes of paint

Spaces for bottles of linseed oil and turpentine

locks in open position

space for brushes and palette knives

*Figure 8*

**TYPICAL SKETCH BOX**

Probably the beginner will be well satisfied with the type of thumb-hole palette which comes with most oil painting sets. (Figure 8.) Such a palette is generally of thin wood in natural finish; it is likely to be rectangular in form and of a size to fit into grooves in the cover of the typical box used by oil painters (often 12 x 16 inches). A palette (and box) of this kind is particularly convenient for outdoor work where equipment must be kept to a minimum.

Thumb-hole palettes are by no means all rectangular; they are of many shapes and sizes. Professionals differ greatly in their choice; some possess several palettes, including small ones for work involving modest quantities of paint, and larger ones for canvases calling for a more generous supply.

The artist who likes to back away from his work frequently and then dash up for a few quick dabs—a sort of hit-and-run technique which has great virtue, especially as a painting nears completion—almost requires some kind of thumb-hole palette. The arm type is popular. (Figure 9.)

*Figure 9*
PALETTE  *This kind of arm palette is ideal for the artist who likes to work rapidly, placing quick dabs on his canvas.*

Yet many other artists, especially when working indoors, prefer a "fixed" or stationary palette. This is merely a sheet of non-absorbent material such as glass, plastic, porcelain or painted wood, laid on top (or forming a part) of a table or artist's taboret. It must be at proper height for ready accessibility; it may be located at left or right—usually the latter—according to one's working habits. Such a table-top palette, together with any adjacent shelves, has the obvious advantage of leaving both hands free. It is also large enough to accommodate many colors, plus cups of thinning medium, bottles of varnish, brushes, palette knives and like tools of the trade, spread out ready for immediate action.

More and more artists are apparently turning to one of the several disposable palettes now on the market. Such a palette consists of a block of paper cut to palette shape and provided with a thumb-hole. (The paper has been previously impregnated so as to make it impervious to paint and mixing mediums.) Held like any other thumb-hole palette, it offers the advantage that at the end of the working day—or at any time, for that matter—the artist can merely strip off and discard the top sheet together with the no-longer-fresh paint which it bears. This exposes a fresh, paint-free surface.

### COLOR OF PALETTE

Many wooden palettes are finished in natural wood color—i.e., cherry, mahogany, birch, etc. Such colors are sometimes needlessly conspicuous and therefore confusing, making it hard for the painter to judge correctly the hues of his paints. It is therefore more logical to use a palette finished in white, or, better yet, neutral gray. (You can, of course, paint or lacquer any wooden palette to either hue.) If glass is used—as on a table top—a sheet of white or neutral gray paper can be laid beneath it. (For that matter, one can buy white or tinted glass.)

### "ALLA PRIMA" PAINTING

As we shall see later, oil paints are often used (by beginner and professional alike) just as they come from the tube. The artist merely squeezes an array of them onto his palette in what seems a logical order—we shall deal with this in the coming chapter—after which he mixes them in small quantities directly upon the palette (or painting) as needed, using his palette knife or brush. Sometimes he dips his brush into each of two or three colors successively, blending them a bit with the brush on either palette or canvas. In other words, for this direct type of work known as *alla prima* painting—or "impasto" if the paint is piled on the canvas thickly—the colors, if not too stiff for ready manipulation, may be employed as purchased. This method has much to recommend it.

### THINNING AND MIXING MEDIUMS

Different paints, even of the same make, vary greatly in consistency. Some when first pressed from the tube seem much thinner than the rest; others appear excessively oily. Now and then it will be found that the liquid vehicle has separated somewhat from the pigment; oily drops may even drip from the tube when opened. Certain paints, on the other hand, may prove gummy or stringy—hard to spread. Some paints dry rapidly once they are squeezed from the tube.

Because of such factors, the artist not infrequently re-mixes his paints upon the palette as needed, thinning them sufficiently to facilitate not only this operation, but the subsequent application and spreading on the canvas. For this purpose, several types of liquid mixing mediums or thinners are obtainable, bottled in suitable form for immediate use. (There are also some in jelly form in tubes.) The most common is rectified turpentine—"turps" in the vocabulary of the painter. (Don't substitute ordinary turpentine from your paint store—it is an inferior product, which among other things, is almost certain to yellow your painting in time.) Refined oil, sun-thickened oil and stand oil are other common mediums (usually intermixed with turpentine, varnish, or both). Your dealer—or better yet, technical books on painting like those to which we have referred—will tell you all about them.

### IT IS HARD TO ADVISE

Unfortunately it is impossible to tell the reader which medium or mediums will best serve his many diverse purposes, especially if the permanence of his paintings is important. If all paints could be made with exactly the same components—which, of course, cannot be done—and if the manufacturers would reveal these components, the problem would be simplified. As it is, some paints call for a quick-drying medium and some for a slow-drying one. Even if the artist knew which was which—and he doesn't—it obviously would be impractical to mix each of a dozen or so colors with a different medium.

Much depends, too, on one's method of working; a painting built up of thin glazes of color over a period of days or even weeks—which allows the successive paint layers to dry—may need a different medium from the *alla prima* type of painting usually finished at one sitting. Another factor to consider is the type of finish desired in the completed work. Some mediums result in highly glossy pictures and others in mat effects.

Inasmuch as most tube colors already contain too much binding mediums (in order to prevent deterioration in the tube), the amount of added medium of an oily nature should be kept at a minimum. Such a medium should also be simple in its chemical make-up; it would obviously be unwise to introduce too many substances in a picture because of possible ultimate unfavorable reaction. A single medium, in other words, should usually be employed throughout any given painting, at least until one becomes quite expert in such matters.

Sometimes the medium is varied from paint layer to paint layer and, if so, the old painter's rule of "fat over lean" should be observed. For the underlayers of a painting, the "lean" and quick-drying turpentine might do, with more oil in the upper layers, following exactly the same procedure as the house painter. But never reverse the process.

### TURPS VS. LINSEED OIL

Speaking of turpentine, many beginners—and some professionals—rely overmuch on it. Employed to excess, it tends to weaken paints with which it is mixed, as it overdilutes the oily binders which hold the pigment particles together. Turps, being a solvent, also tends to dissolve any paint underneath. Too much turpentine causes painted surfaces to dry flat (dull), or to exhibit alternate areas of dullness and gloss, according to the relative amounts of turpentine and oil present. Turps is best for underpainting, and for *alla prima* painting done at one sitting.

An excess of linseed (or other) oil is about as bad as too much turpentine. Oily paints can prove sticky and slow drying, which can be especially annoying if they are used for underpainting to be gone over later with additional coats. Most oils also tend to darken gradually on exposure.

Artists therefore often mix linseed oil and turpentine, or buy in their place one of several ready-prepared mediums which manufacturers claim to be better for all-around work.

### SOME PRACTICAL FORMULAE

Fortunately, the beginner painter is not too much concerned over having his paintings maintain their original appearance forever, so the choice of medium is relatively unimportant to him so long as his paints go on with a minimum of effort and a maximum of pleasing immediate effect.

His present purposes, in other words, can well be served with any one of the following mixtures. Later, if he wishes, he can dig further into the whole thing. One common formula is half turpentine and half linseed oil. Another calls for thirds of turpentine, linseed oil, and damar varnish. Some artists substitute copal or mastic varnish (not picture mastic varnish) for the damar.

*28*

## TURPS AGAIN

Your turpentine will serve a double purpose for, in addition to being a thinner, it is excellent (as we have seen) for cleaning your brushes and palette. Also, used on a rag, it is good for removing unsatisfactory areas of your still wet painting. (A stiff palette knife is invaluable as a scraper in this last connection.)

## DRIERS

In order to speed up the drying of paintings, artists sometimes add to their paints small quantities of "siccative." Use this sparingly, if at all. Employed to excess, it is said to be harmful, impairing the permanence of a painting. A drop of drier (preferably of the type known as "cobalt") to two teaspoonfuls of your painting medium, plus a drop to each two inches of paint as squeezed from the tube, should be ample unless the atmosphere is unusually humid.

You will soon discover that certain colors dry more rapidly than others—experience will teach you which. In most makes, the earth pigments (such as the ochres and umbers) and the lead pigments (including flake white and Naples yellow) dry so quickly that they can serve as driers if you mix them judiciously into your other colors. Raw umber is frequently used in this way. Obviously no siccative should be added to colors which dry well by themselves. Some colors, including most of the blacks, the cadmiums and vermilion, dry slowly. Manufacturers often adjust such varying drying rates so that they are less extreme in their product as you buy it. This makes it impossible for us to give definite rules.

These clip to palette
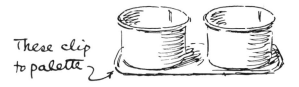

## PALETTE CUPS FOR MEDIUMS

Small cups to contain the mixing mediums (such as turpentine and oil) form a customary part of the painter's equipment. (Double cups may also be purchased. See Figure 10.) Most cups are provided with clips to slip over an edge of the palette, and are held safely by them. Some cups have screw caps to prevent spilling of contents.

*Figure 10*
CUPS FOR MEDIUMS
*Small cups, containing turpentine and oil, are standard articles of equipment for the artist.*

### SOLVENTS

You may like an extra cup for the turpentine, kerosene, mineral spirits or other solvent which you use in rinsing the brush. (We have seen that the brush, whenever loaded with unwanted paint, is dipped in the solvent and then wiped clean.) Don't forget that liquids such as these are highly inflammable!

### PAINT RAGS

Rags are practically indispensable for wiping your brushes. They are also used, dipped in turpentine, for wiping away faulty areas of a painting. Therefore, an ample supply should be always on hand. The less lint they contain, the better. Paper towels also have similar uses. Such rags or towels are highly inflammable when paint laden, so dispose of them accordingly. Spontaneous combustion has often started fires in oil soaked materials.

### PAINTER'S DROP CLOTH

If you plan to work indoors, and wish to protect the floor and rugs, a painter's drop cloth or its equivalent can save a lot of trouble and worry. Your dealer in house paint—sometimes your ten-cent store—can supply this. Newspapers are a common substitute.

### ARTISTS' SMOCKS

These, too, are obviously practical if you wish to protect your clothes. But you must learn to keep out of your paint!

### CHARCOAL, PASTELS, FIXATIVE

Though one's subject matter may be blocked out on the canvas directly in oil paint before any other painting is commenced, it is more customary to sketch it in pencil or charcoal. Charcoal—the "vine" is preferred by many—is also often used for making preliminary studies (on paper) to help the artist decide on his painting composition. If he wishes to make such studies in full color, a set of pastels will also prove convenient. A bottle of fixative (and a mouth atomizer for blowing it on) supplies the means of keeping the charcoal or pastel from smudging. You may prefer one of the new self-spraying plastic fixatives.

## EASELS

You will probably want to do a lot of your work outdoors, in which case the easel you choose should be light in weight and of a type which folds into a reasonably compact package. Yet it must have the strength and rigidity when in use to hold the canvas securely, even in heavy wind. The legs should be pointed. It should also permit the tilting of the canvas at such an angle as to prevent unpleasant and eye-tiring reflections.

In purchasing an easel, look for straight-grain wood—if wood is used—and rustproof hardware. Metal easels—often of aluminum—are becoming increasingly popular. Their light weight and compactness when folded are factors in their favor. Paintbox and easel combinations are also on the market, some of them very practical.

The easel pictured in Figure 11 is one which Jerry Farnsworth has found satisfactory even in the high winds which prevail at his summer school of painting on Cape Cod. The frame which supports the paintbox, with its palette, is a handmade affair (though similar devices are on the market) consisting of three stretcher strips mitered securely to form an equilateral triangle. This slips over the opened easel to support the box, which in turn weighs down the whole thing. Some painters prefer their box within easier reach on a separate folding rack or stool.

*Figure 11*

EASEL  *Don't make a hasty choice, because very clever models have come onto the market in recent years.*

## STOOL

For outdoor work, you may want to sit on a sturdy but lightweight folding stool (Figure 12), though many painters always stand. Sometimes a second stool is substituted for an easel, the painting propped against it. Again, as just mentioned, a second stool is used as a rest to support the paintbox; some keep their palette on such a stool.

## PAINTBOX

A paintbox—"sketch box" in the dealer's terminology—while not absolutely essential, is certainly convenient. As stated at the start, you may wish to simplify your purchasing problem by buying such a box fitted ready for use— an "oil color set." Many beginners do this, gradually adding other equipment or making substitutions.

FOLDING STOOL

*Figure 12A*

STOOL  *This folding stool is handy when you paint outdoors and want a place to rest your palette, your canvas, or yourself.*

Frederic Taubes, in his *Oil Painting for the Beginner* (Watson-Guptill), offers the student this twelve-color basic list as a starter:

| | |
|---|---|
| White lead (flake white) | Venetian red |
| Prussian blue | Cadmium red light |
| Ultramarine blue | Alizarin crimson |
| Viridian green (chromoxide green transparent) | Burnt sienna |
| | Burnt umber |
| Yellow ochre | Ivory black |
| Cadmium yellow light | |

STANLEY WOODWARD'S PALETTE

This noted marine painter, in his book *Marine Painting* (Watson-Guptill), presents a larger list—his own working palette of eighteen colors—though he by no means uses all of these on any one canvas:

| | |
|---|---|
| Zinc white | Rose madder |
| Zinc yellow | Alizarin crimson |
| Cadmium yellow medium | Viridian green |
| Cadmium orange | Cerulean blue |
| Cadmium red lightest | Cobalt blue |
| Yellow ochre | Manganese |
| Raw sienna | Ultramarine |
| Burnt umber | Indian red |
| Burnt sienna | Black |

A fifty percent mixture of turpentine and linseed oil is Woodward's usual thinning medium.

It probably makes little difference just what selection of colors you choose at the beginning, though all of the above lists are recommended. As time goes on, you will find that you are neglecting certain colors while using others in considerable quantity. Friends will tell you of some of their favorites, too, and it will be fun to try them. If you are inquisitive enough to dig into the chemistry of the matter, you will find some of the books which we mentioned earlier very helpful. In your reading, you will discover facts like the following:

The red color, vermilion, has fallen somewhat into disfavor. It is sometimes blackened by the direct rays of the sun. Emerald green is basic copper arsenate and very poisonous; it should not be mixed with the vermilions or cadmiums; it is darkened by impure atmosphere. (Many colors besides emerald green are poisonous to some degree—all of the lead colors, for example—so don't eat them!) Flake whites are the most used of the whites but are lead pigments and also sullied by impure atmosphere. Zinc white is not so blackened and is absolutely permanent, but is less opaque than flake white. Colors containing too much oil tend to darken eventually because of yellowing of oil.

In connection with all of this, scout around at your art supply dealer's. Tell him about your problems. He will tip you off as to the most popular colors, or, for that matter, other good items of equipment. Get to know him well, for he can prove a valuable friend. And follow such creative art magazines as *American Artist;* their editorial pages will introduce you to many working methods, while their advertising pages will keep you posted on the latest and best in equipment.

That winds up for now the matter of selecting materials. Whether you buy a five dollar "set" at your dealer's (I have seen them as low as two-fifty and not wholly to be despised!) or invest from twenty-five to a hundred dollars (the latter amount is extreme), you have at least made the initial step; you are ready for days and days of the thrills (and disappointments) of trying to become a painter.

# Chapter 2
## SETTING THE PALETTE

WHENEVER I WATCH artists at work, or whenever I visit painting classes, I am struck by one thing: artists are highly individual in the way they "set" or "lay" their selected colors on their palettes. Almost every artist has his own pet arrangement. Some teachers are very dogmatic on the subject, stating to their students, "Do it *this* way. It is the only right way."

I am not going to tell you any one way to do it, for there is no one way which is always best. I shall show you instead a few common ways which seem sensible for the beginner and let you choose for yourself. The thing which really counts is this: once you decide on a given arrangement you will do well to stick to it indefinitely (unless experience shows that you can improve it), because you can save a great deal of time—and painting hours are precious!—if you fall into the habit of always having each hue in the same place so that when you want it you will automatically thrust your brush in its direction.

Not that a painter *always* sticks to one precise arrangement. Sometimes, in fact, he even varies his selection of colors. It is obvious, for instance, that for painting the brilliant hues of sunlit autumn foliage he may require colors quite different from those needed for the dull effects of a rainy day. What I am advocating is that you should always keep your basic colors—including white and black—in the same positions, and if you

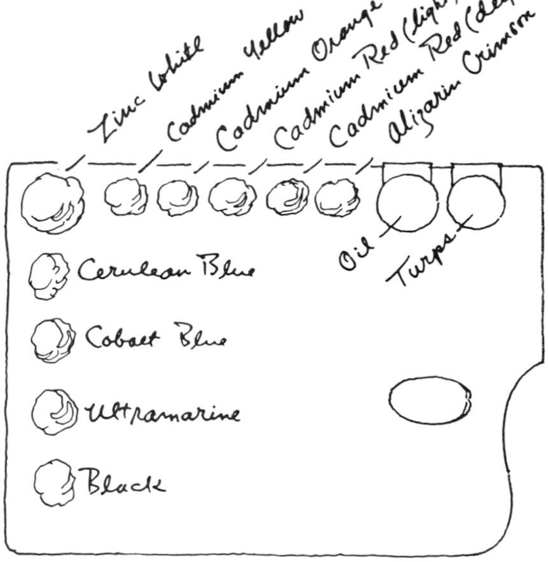

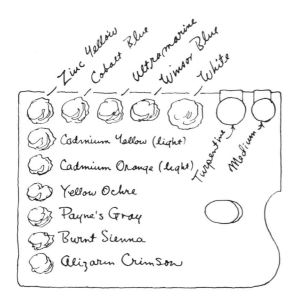

*Figure 13*

COLORS   *Here is a typical assortment for a start.*

add others for some particular job, they, too, should go in their own places.

Figure 13 shows one common, and highly recommended, arrangement. Here the cups for oil and turpentine are at the upper right—out of the way of the colors but accessible when needed. White—and a large amount of it—is at the upper left. The cool colors run down the left-hand edge (with black at the bottom) and the warm colors across the top.

As Figure 14 we offer a palette presented by amateur painter Lawrence V. Burton in his book *Week-end Painter* (McGraw-Hill). He also illustrates in this book various other arrangements, according to the number of colors needed. His own palette (16 x 20 inches) is somewhat more complex, embracing seventeen colors and white. Incidentally, Burton makes a good point when he says, "Don't be niggardly when laying out your colors; neither be extravagant. Only experience will tell you how much . . . to squeeze out."

*Figure 14*

COLORS   *Another way of "setting the palette."*

This matter of palette size is important. If the painter's palette is too small to accommodate adequate amounts of the colors needed, he feels baffled at times. But a large palette is too heavy to hold for long and so calls for some sort of special support such as a stool, stand, or an easel of the type which can be adjusted to a horizontal position.

When a palette is large enough to permit it, colors are sometimes placed down the right side as well. This is illustrated by Figure 15, which shows one of the ways in which Frederic Taubes sets his palette, in this case a table top. Taubes, by the way, offers a very practical hint: "A paint as it comes from the tube may sometimes prove too oily. To remove an excess of oil, spread the paint on an absorbent paper such as newspaper. After a few minutes the excess will have been taken up."

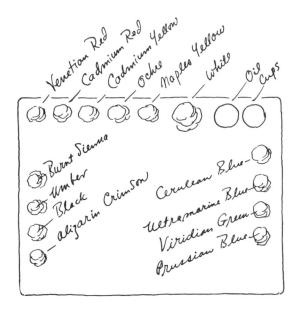

*Figure 15*
COLORS *Frederic Taubes recommends this choice.*

*Figure 16*
COLORS *A list suggested by Jerry Farnsworth.*

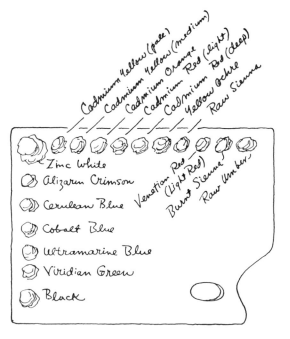

Figure 16, based on an illustration in Jerry Farnsworth's book, *Portrait and Figure Painting,* shows a paint arrangement which he recommends to his students. "It will be noted in the arrangement pictured here," says Farnsworth, "that from zinc white to raw umber we have the warm colors, from very light to very dark. On the other side of the white we have three blues: ultramarine, cobalt, and cerulean (the latter necessary out-of-doors, but not always indoors), along with alizarin crimson, viridian and black." This palette has been used by hundreds of students.

In some palette arrangements, the artist follows much the sequence of the visible portions of the spectrum, as exemplified in our color wheel, Figure 20. In another wholly different arrangement he places side by side those colors which he is most likely to employ in frequent mixture. Yellow and blue, for example, may be adjacently located if greens are likely to be called for. The same is true of blue and red for the mixture of violet. This thought helps to demonstrate that even if a palette arrangement appears at first glance to be illogical, more than likely it has been carefully worked out according to the artist's specific needs based on long experience. The portrait artist must mix soft, rich flesh colors; the flower painter needs a wealth of vivid hues. These would be assembled accordingly. Neither the same colors, to repeat, nor the same arrangements, can suit every taste or purpose.

ON THE USE OF BLACK

Some teachers tell their students, "Never use black. Keep it off your palette!" And it is true that nature seldom shows us tones even approaching the jet black of undiluted oil paint. Anything black which we see out-of-doors is veiled by atmosphere, reflects the sky or is otherwise modified in tone; so that if black paint is used in its interpretation it must be similarly modified.

Black can be very useful, however, if employed with discrimination. And it seems foolish to have to mix approximate blacks from your other pigments if you can get satisfactory results from black itself.

If you don't use black, you may substitute Payne's gray, or you can mix satisfactory approximations of black by combining such colors as cadmium red deep and ultramarine blue. Almost any dark red, yellow and blue paint, for that matter, will mix together to give you an approximation of black.

No paint, by the way, is pure black. Ivory black, the best-liked black, is usually brownish, as you can easily demonstrate by lightening it greatly with white. Lampblack can similarly be proved a dark, neutral blue. But all this doesn't matter, for brown-blacks and blue-blacks are what nature often calls for (but seldom in full dark value!).

To sum up, be *very* sparing in the use of black; you can quite easily get along without it.

(As a matter of fact, any exceptionally dark or powerful color, used in excess, can cause havoc. Prussian blue, for example, always calls for sympathetic handling because of its exceptionally dark value and strong hue even when greatly diluted. Some finished paintings by beginners look like advertisements of Prussian blue! So employ it with care if at all, or it will overpower your other colors.)

### WHITE

Even white, the most used paint of all, can cause unpleasant, chalky effects. As to choice of white, zinc white is preferred by many to white lead (flake white). The newer titanium white, though lacking the test of time, is growing more popular daily. But all are capable of unnatural, chalky effects under some circumstances, as you will soon discover.

Just as few things in nature are black, few are white, so white paint must almost invariably be at least tinted with other paints. But now and then you will want little touches of pure white, as for tiny highlights, for instance, so get the habit of keeping your white paint on your palette clean—this isn't easy to do. (This advice goes for all light paints.)

In short, you will gradually discover that *it matters less what paints you have on your palette than what you learn to do with them.*

### CLEANING YOUR PALETTE

How long shall you leave your paints in place? That depends entirely on circumstances and your own way of working. Some painters scrape and wipe their palettes clean at the end of every painting session, and I recommend that you do this, at least for a time. In a couple of days paint may set enough to call for vigorous scraping or considerable use of turps or other solvent. Some painters, however, merely wipe the center of the palette clean every day or so, letting the rest go for days and even weeks without cleaning, adding fresh colors as needed, until the accumulation crowds them into action. Under such circumstances they may need to soak the paint with solvent—even paint remover—before it can be wholly scraped away. In any case, keep the center of your palette clean at all times, so wipe it frequently with your paint rag. As a closing thought, when you again apply your colors to a palette after cleaning it, it is excellent practice to rub it over first with a thin coating of linseed oil.

# *Chapter 3*

## BRUSH AND
## KNIFE
## EXERCISES

PERHAPS I SHOULD say to you at this time, "Once you have set your palette you are ready to paint a picture. Merely use your brush and knife in the most natural manner and proceed with your work." For it's a fact that there is no one approved way of holding and manipulating these and your other tools. I have watched many artists at work and they are even more individual in their painting habits than in their handwriting.

Some of them—a very limited minority—operate in a very detailed manner, using fine brushes, perhaps on a small canvas. Often they sit rather than stand. As a rule they hold these brushes much as they would a pen or pencil, grasping them near the metal ferrule. They may, at times at least, rest the hand on the canvas for greater accuracy and detail. If the canvas is wet, they may use an artist's mahlstick as a hand support. (This is a plain round stick, often telescopic, made of wood or metal and tipped with rubber at one end. Held in the left hand—by the right-handed painter—with the tip at the right edge or top of the canvas or touching any uncompleted area of the picture—or, for that matter, resting on the easel or elsewhere—the mahlstick affords a hand support well adapted to certain techniques.

A majority of artists, on the other hand, abhor at least some of these practices, claiming that they will result in labored, tight work. They believe that only by standing well back from their canvas, and grasping a reasonably long-handled brush at or near the small end, can they see their painting as a whole and execute it with the needed freedom, speed, and breadth.

In these matters you will unquestionably be wise to follow the majority. But don't feel that you must ape their practices during every painting moment. While it is generally felt that one should stand rather than sit, there will be times when you will be only too glad to be off your feet. On occasion, too, you may wish to use a brush technique which will demand a scrubbing or rotating motion impossible without a firm grip on the brush. Or your subject may call for a decisiveness of line difficult to obtain unless you hold the brush near—though not necessarily at—the metal ferrule. What I am saying, in other words, is that in this matter of brush and knife handling the painter has reasonable license.

In your first paintings, though, don't fall into the especially bad habit of staying too close to your work as you execute it or you may later find this habit hard to break. When you work too close, your eye is almost certain to focus on a few square inches at a time, with the result that you may be tempted to over-develop this limited area, and then the next such area, and the next, thus losing the breadth of effect—the bigness of conception and boldness of execution—without which almost any painting is doomed to failure.

As a starter, why not experiment with each brush for a bit, and with your knives as well? Learn what kinds of *lines* you can make. Discover how strokes may be combined to form *tones*. See what sort of *textures* you can develop. At the moment, don't think too much about color; we'll soon get to that. Squeeze out four or five colors: some white, perhaps some burnt umber, possibly some blue or green. You need only enough colors to give you a little variety in value and hue. For this first practice, use your paint just as it comes from the tube unless you find it unworkable; in this case, add a minimum of medium.

*Exercise 1: Lines*
With each of your brushes in turn, carry some single strokes across your canvas, not unlike those below, but much longer. Use paint generously. Don't be disturbed by the ridges of paint which may squeeze out along the edges of a stroke, or by the way the line breaks to show some canvas through as the brushful of paint becomes exhausted, giving the result

known as "dry brush." These effects are characteristic of oil painting, and often are created intentionally. Do some lines with the flat sides of your brushes, others with the thinner edges. Try light paint, medium paint, dark paint. Tip the bristles at different angles to the canvas. Vary your pressure. Make wavy lines, broken lines, zigzag lines. Invent lines of your own. Ultimately you will need them all.

As you work with your brush, you may find that you will want to turn it over, or up on edge, every little while in order to use the paint which accumulates. That's quite all right!

### BROKEN COLOR

In some of these lines, use a single color. In others, dip your brush into two or more colors so that, as you paint, these colors will automatically blend somewhat yet each will remain visible in places. Such accidental effects as you obtain in this way can be used very tellingly at times.

### Exercise 2: Tones

Most painting is tonal rather than linear, so experiment with various ways of combining brush strokes to fill areas with tone. Let long straight strokes slightly overlap. Or crisscross some strokes, perhaps later brushing them out into comparatively uniform tone. Interweave or overlap various short strokes to form tone, with or without small bare areas of the canvas showing between them. In brief, combine short straight strokes, short curved strokes, short wavy or broken strokes; then do longer strokes having similar variety. Make some smooth, uniform tones. Grade some

44

tones from light to dark, some from dark to light, and some from one color to another, in each case striving for a uniform gradation. Paint light lines or dots into dark areas. In other words, be inventive.

**DABS OR BLOBS OF COLOR**

Tones are often built up by merely touching a paint-laden brush to the canvas repeatedly to "print" many dabs of color side by side. These may or may not overlap. Often several colors are used in this way, the different colors more or less intermingling but still retaining something of their original hues.

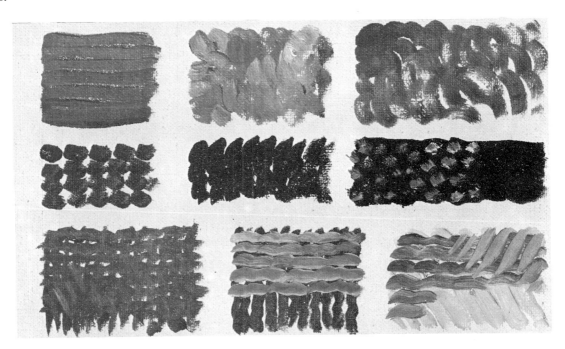

*Exercise 3: Thinned paint*

For early work on a canvas, the paint is often considerably thinned (usually with turpentine) for laying the foundation (underpainting) for the work to follow. The paint must not, of course, be thin enough to run, but it can approach that state. Experiment with paint thus diluted with turpentine to different consistencies. Then thin some with oil instead of turps so as to get the "feel" and appearance of both types of paint. Next try a medium of half turps, half oil.

*Exercise 4: Wiping off*

If, when an artist is painting a picture, a certain passage fails to "arrive," he doesn't fool with it too long. He scrapes it with his palette knife, or wipes it off (in whole or in part) with his paint rag. His finger is a good tool for this; he shoves his index finger into the folded rag to form a sort of brush. Then he gathers the rest of the rag into his hand to keep it out of the paint and wipes into the offensive area. He may want to dip the cloth-enclosed finger in the turpentine first in order to cleanse the area sufficiently.

Paint a few areas and then experiment with them in this manner, wiping some of them away entirely and leaving others to paint over again later. These wiped lines sometimes become a part of the final technique.

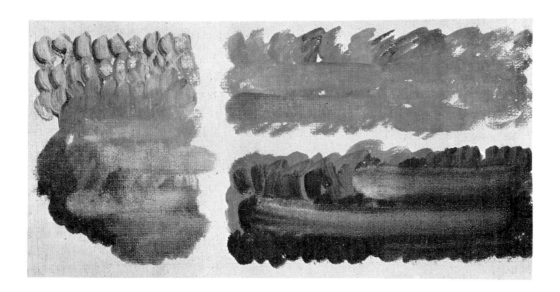

*Exercise 5: Painting into drying paint*

Much work is painted "wet-in-wet," the artist completing a sketch at one sitting. Often, however, it is necessary or desirable to come back to a painting the next day, or for several days. This means painting into areas which are already partially dry. The effects which result are often quite different from those painted in any other way. As an experiment in this direction, coat some fairly large areas with different varieties of tone and let them partially dry. In a day or two—or even in a few hours—paint back into them. If such areas are quite dry, by the way, they often receive subsequent brushwork more sympathetically if they are first coated with a bit of medium or retouching varnish. This is especially true if they have dried flat and dull. (The medium or varnish may be sprayed on with a fixative blower.) Experiment!

### Exercise 6: Knife painting

Now do with your painting knives much the same as you have done with your brushes. (See Figure 17, but don't try to copy it!) Draw wide lines with the flat or point of a knife, fine lines with its edge. Dab on blobs of thick paint. Use a knife as a spreader to cover large canvas areas, and as a scraper of tone already in place. In short, try everything which comes to mind, remembering that, as with your brushes, every trick which you

*Figure 17*
**KNIFE EXERCISES**  *Your knives, like your brushes, are most versatile. Don't fail to explore all possibilities for utilizing them.*

learn now will have a thousand later applications. Your knives may seem clumsy tools at first but with practice they can become amazingly fast and effective.

Obviously the lines or tones which you make during these experiments, whether done with knives or brushes, won't look like much. That doesn't matter at all. The only thing which counts is what you learn.

This is a good time, by the way, for you to examine original oil painting inch by inch to study the handling of other painters. When an area has been worked over repeatedly, you may not be able to determine just how it was done, but you can often pick up ideas to help you in your own work with brush or knife.

### A WORD OF WARNING

While today's painters often make use of such thick brush and knife paint application (impasto) as the above exercises include, experts tell us that if permanence is sought, such thick coats of paint, or many repeated coats, should be avoided. They are almost certain to crack ultimately or otherwise deteriorate.

# Chapter 4

## GETTING TO KNOW YOUR COLORS

ONCE YOU HAVE assembled your materials and done a few preliminary brush and knife exercises like those suggested in the previous chapter, you may be impatient to paint your first picture. While there can be no great harm in immediately making this initial attempt, you will probably save much time and trouble in the end and advance on a firmer basis if, as a preliminary, you give a few hours to gaining a speaking acquaintance with each of your different paints. Not only is it essential for you to fix in your mind a correct impression of every one of your colors as it appears fresh from the tube, but you will want to discover how this color looks when lightened with white, darkened with black, and mixed in turn with each of your other colors. In concentrating on this, you can simultaneously gain a fair grasp of at least the basic principles and practices of mixing, matching and applying colors.

I believe that you will find the following exercise fun, for you have already discovered that the mere blending of your paints proves most fascinating and revealing. These exercises may be done on any white canvas of convenient size; it need not be of high quality. Save each sheet and fasten it to the wall where you can study it frequently.

At the risk of giving you a few minutes of mental indigestion before the fun of experimenting with your paints, I interrupt our thought just long enough to interject a few definitions. You probably don't like definitions and technical terms any better than I do, but occasionally a few prove necessary.

Unfortunately, the terms common to the field of color can prove very confusing. The physicist, dealing with color in the form of light, utilizes a highly scientific vocabulary. The psychologist, concerned with visual and mental impressions of color, has another terminology, equally erudite. The painter prefers his own language, somewhat more simple, yet scarcely less strange to the layman's ears. And even the painter is not always consistent. Many of his words, such as "shade," "tint," "tone," and "value," have a variety of meanings.

If these variations were confined to terminology, it would be bad enough, but the student of painting is confronted with more vital differences. Referring again to the physicist, his "primary," or basic, colors from which all other colors can be created—remember he is dealing with light—are red, green, and blue (blue-violet). To the psychologist, I understand that the primaries are red, yellow, green, blue, black, and white. The painter's primaries—*our* primaries as we work with color in the form of paint—are generally understood to be red, yellow, and blue, though painters don't even agree on this!

So the terms I shall use may or may not be the ones to which you are accustomed. Certainly some of them would not be the choice of the scientist, but I believe most of them have general acceptance in the field of painting.

### HUE

Color possesses three qualities or attributes of which the most outstanding is hue. Webster defines "hue" as "that attribute in respect to which colors may be described as red, yellow, green or blue, or as an intermediate between two of these. . . ." In the layman's language, the word "hue" relates to the *name* of a color. An apple is red; red is the hue of that apple. We can alter the hue of a color by mixing another color with it. If we mixed red paint with yellow paint we produce orange paint. That is a change in hue.

*50*

### BRILLIANCE OR VALUE

Webster defines "brilliance" as "that one of the three attributes of a color . . . in respect to which it may be classed as equivalent to some member of the series of grays ranging from black . . . to white; roughly the degree of resemblance to white or difference from black."

Many artists prefer, in place of the term "brilliance," the word "value." It is by value that we are able to discriminate between light red and dark red. By mixing a color with something lighter or darker than itself we change its value.

### SATURATION, CHROMA, OR INTENSITY

Coming to our third color quality, and again quoting Webster, "Saturation is that attribute in respect to which colors may be differentiated as being higher or lower in degree of vividness of hue; that is, as differing in degree from gray." As "saturation" refers to vividness or distinctness of hue, the more gray we mix in a color the less saturated it becomes.

Some artists substitute the word "chroma" for "saturation." Webster tells us that "chroma" characterizes a color qualitatively without reference to its brilliance (value), thus embracing both hue and saturation.

Still more in use by the artist in this connection is the word "intensity," so this is the term we shall employ in the coming chapters, despite the fact that many authorities don't recognize "intensity" as a color term. It at least has the merit of defining itself. Simply stated, some colors are strong and some weak; the quality by which we distinguish between them is called "intensity." We can change the intensity of a color by mixing it with something which tends to dull or gray it. We can change intensity without changing value or hue by adding neutral gray of equal value.

### NORMAL COLORS, TINTS, AND SHADES

A color in its full, natural strength may be called a "normal color," or a "color of normal value." If lighter we call it a "tint"; if darker, a "shade." In this sense, it is wrong to refer to "a light shade" of a color, or to "a dark tint" of a color. Remember that tints are all light, shades are all dark.

*51*

*Paul Puzinas:* WATERFRONT VIEW  *The color scheme in this painting is dominated by green with hints of its complement, pink. Notice how notes of pink appear throughout the painting—in the debris, in the building on the pier, and even in the sky. At points, the pinks blend with the greens to produce shades of browns and grays.*

The word "tone" is another of varied and complex meaning. Webster offers this: "Color quality or value; any tint or shade of color; any modification of a chromatic or achromatic color with respect to brilliance or saturation; also, the color which appreciably modifies a hue or white or black; as, a bright, dark, or light *tone* of blue; the gray walls took on a greenish *tone;* the soft *tones* of the old marble." As to painting, Webster adds this thought on the word "tone": "The general effect due to the combination of light and shade, together with color;—commonly implying harmony; as, this picture has *tone.*"

So much by way of definition. Now let's get down to exercises.

*Exercise 7: Hue and name*

Squeeze onto your canvas a bit of each of your colors, spreading it about with your palette knife or brush to cover thoroughly an area measuring a square inch or more. (If you arrange these in a horizontal row, you can combine this Exercise 7 with Exercise 9.) It will prove convenient, for ease in comparison, if you group your areas of each general hue together. In other words, group all of your reds, then all your yellows, etc. Alongside each hue write in pencil its name (as it appears on the tube) in order to learn to associate each color with its correct name. Try to form a permanent mental image of both hue and name so that whenever you want some of this color in the future you will know which tube contains it.

*Exercise 8: Drying test*

We have seen that some paints dry much more rapidly than others. It is helpful to gain a general idea of at least the surface drying qualities of every one of your paints. Therefore, test with your finger every few hours each painted area used for Exercise 7. Later, add penciled notes to indicate whether it proves quick, medium or slow to dry.

*Exercise 9: Normal colors, tints, shades*

For your present purpose, each of the colors before you might be considered a "normal" color, that term being sometimes loosely applied to colors —especially the more brilliant ones—just as they come from the tube. Some painting will be done with your colors in this natural form. Often, however, it will be necessary to lighten, darken, or otherwise so modify them as to create a greater variety of hues to approximate the myriad colors of nature.

There are several ways in which you can obtain on your white, or nearly white canvas, tints of each of your colors. (1) You can dilute each paint with turpentine or other thinner; the more thinner you add, the lighter the tint will of course become, because the color will gradually change from opacity through translucency to transparency, allowing the light canvas to show through more and more clearly. (2) You can brush the paint so thin that the canvas shows through plainly. (3) You can blend in some white paint—here your palette knife will prove helpful. This is the most common way of creating tints. (4) You can add light paint of some other color, although when you do this you tend to confuse the issue; you are not only creating a tint but you are simultaneously changing the color's hue so it really becomes another color rather than a tint of the original color.

Similarly, you can obtain shades by adding black to each of your normal colors. (You can also add darks of other hues, but they will of course somewhat modify the original hues.)

As Exercise 9, paint a row of squares (each an inch or so in size) horizontally across the middle of a canvas, one for each of your colors just as it comes from the tube (or use the areas painted as Exercise 7). As before, group the reds; also, the yellows, blues, greens, and browns. Above this row, paint a second row of squares in which every color is somewhat lightened by the addition of white. This will give you a series of tints. Above this, add a third row in which the colors are still further diluted with white, creating even lighter tints. Above this, add, if you wish, a fourth row (or more) containing constantly increasing amounts of white.

Now for some shades. Below the original rows of colors paint a second row, with each color somewhat darkened by intermixing a little black, and below this a third row with each color considerably darkened. Below this you may want to add a fourth and perhaps a fifth row of increasingly darker shades.

### ANALYSIS

You will now begin to see what a variety of colors is obtainable through even this simple addition of white or black to each of your normal colors. Some interesting comparisons will also be evident. For instance, if you study your two series showing what we have loosely called normal colors and tints, and normal colors and shades, you will observe among other things that normal colors vary greatly in tone, some being quite light and others quite dark. For example, yellow in its normal form—the purest, brightest yellow on your palette—is light in tone—really a tint in relation to most normal colors. Therefore, as you add the white to yellow to create a series of yellowish tints, these will vary only slightly one from another. On the contrary, in the case of a paint which is normally dark—deep blue or violet, for instance—as you add the white to create tints, you will discover a very noticeable difference from area to area. Whereas a light tint of yellow will look quite similar in value to the normal yellow paint, a light tint of deep blue or violet will look very different from the normal deep blue or violet.

Now study your areas of shades. Here the yellow will change very rapidly in tone as the black is added to make it darker. The chances are that a dark shade of yellow will have an appearance which you would scarcely recognize as yellow, yet, strictly speaking, it is. In the case of your deep blue or violet, there will be far less difference in your shade squares. Try to get all such differences in mind (as revealed by your painted areas) so that if you wish to represent a certain tint or shade when working from nature you will know just what paint will give it to you through the addition of white or black only.

I wish that I could sufficiently impress upon you the importance of trying to memorize the fundamental appearances of these tints and shades which you can obtain by the simple addition of white or black to each of your colors. It is a task, of course, but an extremely rewarding one.

If we follow the next logical step, and mix one color with another, plus black and white, the number of color variations which we can create approaches infinity. All of these are at your command. But before we explore this fascinating chromatic field in this manner, let's lay our colored paints to one side for a few minutes in order to concentrate on the scarcely less remarkable range of tones which can be created through the mixture of white and black alone.

White is obviously the lightest value we have in our paints, and black the darkest. (See Figure 18, A.) Between the two lies an enormous range of values. Halfway from white to black is a "half black" often referred to as "middle value" or "neutral gray." Similarly, halfway between white and this half black is a "quarter black" or "three-quarter white," and halfway between half black and black is a "three-quarter black" or "one-quarter white."

55

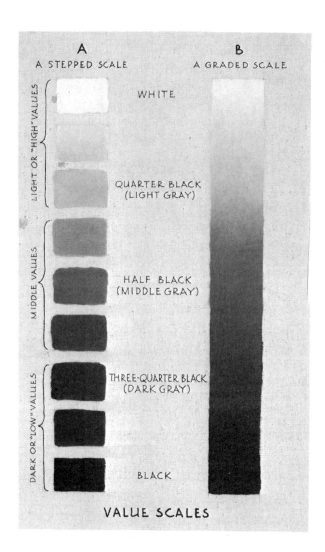

Figure 18
**VALUE SCALES** *Tones of light and dark are fully as important as color. Such scales as these help you to understand them.*

We might go on with such subdivisions almost indefinitely. In our diagram we have added four additional intermediate tones so that we finally have nine, giving us a sequence of eight graduated steps from white to black. (I hope it is clear that the actual number of steps in such a scale doesn't matter in the least; all such groupings of tones are purely arbitrary ones devised only to help us learn to recognize different degrees of light and dark as we see them in nature and as we interpret them in our painting. Obviously values in nature are seldom arranged in any such set manner.)

*56*

*Exercise 10: Stepped value scale*

If you are to develop a keen perception of differences in tone, whether in nature or in your work—and you should—the painting of one or more white to black "value scales" similar to that at A should help. The method is self-evident.

### YOU CAN MEASURE TONES

You can think of such a value scale as a sort of ruler for measuring or judging the degree of light or dark in any given tone, much as a yardstick is employed to measure feet and inches. Look at some tone in nature, compare it with your scale, and you can tell just about what its value is. (Nature, however, has values in brilliant sunshine which are much lighter and brighter than either your white canvas or your lightest and brightest colors. You must realize at the start that it will forever be impossible for you to duplicate with your paints the extreme values of hues of nature; at best you will be able to obtain an approximation—a reasonably satisfactory impression or illusion.)

*Exercise 11: Graded value scale*

At this point it is also helpful—not only in making you still more aware of value differences, but in aiding you to learn to manipulate your paints —to paint a graded scale such as we suggest at B. This is exactly like scale A except that the component values have been so blended as to give a consistent gradation from white to black, rather than a series of somewhat artificial steps.

*Figure 19*
**COLOR MIXTURE**
*Here is a logical way to learn how to create hundreds of hues and values from the dozen or so colors on your palette.*

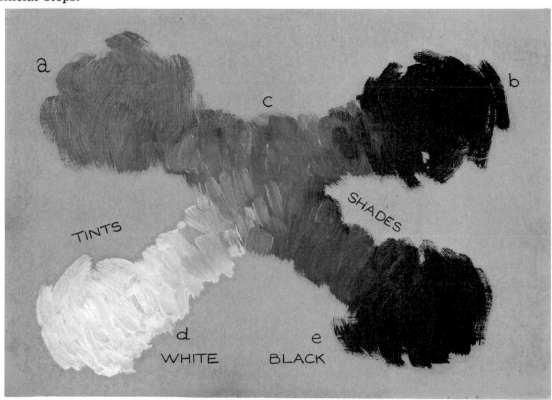

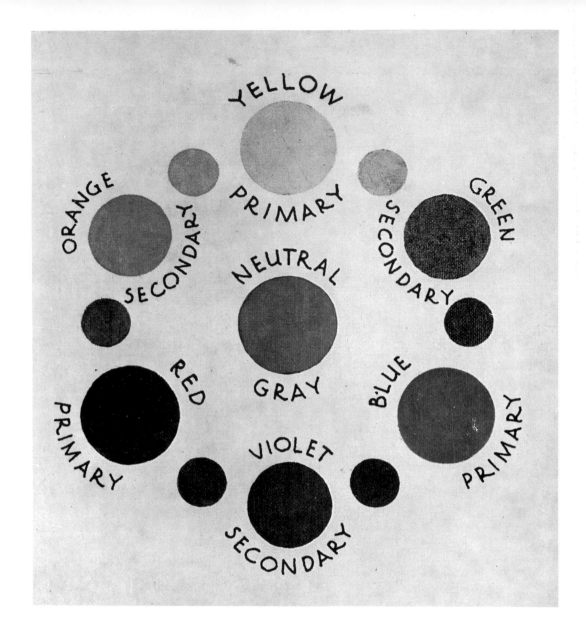

You have now (Exercise 9) mixed each of your tube colors with white and black to obtain tints and shades; you have also (Exercises 10 and 11) mixed your white with black to give you a wide variety of values. Some students find it revealing as a next step to make a graded value scale for each tube color, following the same procedure used for the white-to-black scale at B—one must add both white and black to each color. Do this if you wish; it should prove time well spent. Save all results for further study and comparison.

58

*Exercise 12: Mixing one color with another*

When it comes to mixing pairs of colors in order to discover what the two will yield, there is no best way; any experiments which you perform will help you to gain acquaintance with your colors. The more systematic your procedure, however, the more you will profit. Obviously your main purpose is to learn how to obtain from your dozen or so paints the numerous colors which will ultimately be needed when, in painting your pictures, you wish to interpret or approximate nature's multitudinous hues.

Figure 19 suggests one logical procedure: Squeeze out a small amount of any color (a) and, three or four inches away, a like amount of any second color (b). Then, using a stiff brush or palette knife, bring the two together (c) and intermix them quite thoroughly. To extend your experiment further, blend a bit of white (d) and black (e) into the lower edges of the color just created, extending tones downward to left and right as indicated. Thus you will not only see what, through admixture, the two colors yield in the way of a third color, but you will discover how this third color will appear in a full gamut of values ranging from light tints to dark shades. Repeat this exercise (or any similar one of your own invention) with many pairs of paints. (You may eventually want to go even further, experimenting with mixtures of three or four paints.)

#### A FASCINATING DISCOVERY

This mixing of colors can prove as entertaining as it is informative. By a sort of magic you will create from your limited number of original hues a large number of new hues; remember that in theory, if not in practice, all colors can be mixed from the three paint primaries, red, yellow and blue, plus black and white.

You will note interesting things about these mixtures. For example, one pair of bright colors (such as red and yellow) will mix to produce a third bright color (orange), while another pair of equally bright colors (such as red and green) will, on the contrary, produce a dull color (gray or drab-brown). Why?

#### COLOR WHEEL

Such differences can perhaps best be noted, understood, and memorized by referring to (or, better yet, by making) a gadget known as a color wheel. (See Figure 20.) Different authorities recommend different wheels; it matters little which you make. Most such wheels are based on the fact repeatedly mentioned that it is possible to mix almost any colors from the three so-called primaries—red, yellow and blue, plus black and white. (You will recall that physicists, working with light, use as their primaries red, green and blue-violet. Don't let this confuse you—you can't get the same results with pigments as physicists can with light.) This is as true of inks or dyes as it is of paints. The color plates in this book, for example, no matter what their apparent number of colors, were printed entirely from four inks: red, yellow, blue and black, white being supplied by the paper. Examine these color pages under a magnifying glass and you can doubtless detect (especially along the edges) dots of each of these basic hues.

*Exercise 13: Making a color wheel*
It will pay you to make a color wheel of your own, perhaps on the order of that shown. First rough out in pencil on your canvas a circle six or seven inches wide—or of any convenient size. Around this, pencil small circles as in Figure 20.

### PRIMARY COLORS

Start by applying, in the positions indicated on Figure 20, small areas of your primary colors. You may not have a red as clear and bright as could be desired, but choose your "reddest" red—one which is towards neither orange nor violet. Paint on your circle where indicated an area of this red, full strength. Next choose your purest yellow, and add an area of that. Do the same with blue. (Some manufacturers offer "spectrum" paints especially made for this type of color study.)

### SECONDARY COLORS

If you mix together primary red and primary yellow they will give orange; primary yellow and primary blue will give green; and primary blue and primary red will give violet. These three new colors thus obtained —orange, green and violet—are often called the "secondary" colors. Apply them in the positions indicated in Figure 20.

### INTERMEDIATE COLORS

Continuing in the same manner by mixing the three primaries and three

*Sherman Hoeflich:* ARCY SUR CURE   *Here is an effective example of how colors may be used in a painting to develop unity. The colors of the buildings are picked up in the sky and water. Notice how analogous colors—red and orange, blue and green—are employed to further this sense of unity. Practice with colors so that you can use them imaginatively too!*

secondaries, you can obtain six intermediate hues, namely: red-orange, yellow-orange, yellow-green, blue-green, blue-violet, and red-violet. These six colors are sometimes erroneously referred to as "tertiary" colors. Strictly speaking, this word "tertiary" is a misnomer when applied to a color thus mixed from a primary and a secondary, for the dictionary tells us that "a tertiary is a color produced by a mixture of two secondary colors." Let us, therefore, yield to the dictionary and refer to this third group of hues as "intermediates."

Don't be unduly concerned with these names; in themselves they mean very little. But paint the colors on your wheel, for when all twelve are arranged around an arbitrary circle such as we illustrate, they give us—to repeat—a very useful instrument which is based to some degree on the visible elements of nature's chromatic spectrum.

Now let us see how we can utilize this wheel.


### ANALOGOUS COLORS

Colors which are adjoining or adjacent to any one of the primaries on the color wheel are obviously somewhat similar in character or of one family. We refer to these as "analogous" or "related" colors. Red, red-orange, and red-violet are analogous, as they all contain red. So are blue, blue-green, and blue-violet; they all contain blue. *Because of their common factor, analogous colors of any one family harmonize esthetically among themselves and so can usually be employed together safely.*


### COMPLEMENTARY COLORS

Colors which lie directly opposite each other on our arbitrary wheel (typical pairs are red and green, yellow and violet, blue and orange) are, on the other hand, dissimilar in character—to an extent inharmonious, at least in their natural state. They do not belong to the same family; they possess no self-evident chromatic similarity. (Read, however, what we say on pages 79 and 80.) Such opposite colors are called "complementaries."

These *opposite colors are the ones which tend to annihilate each other when mixed together*. We have seen that red mixed with green produces gray. Similarly, yellow mixed with violet, or blue mixed with orange, neutralize one another. And so it is with any opposite pair on our little chart, such as blue-violet and yellow-orange, red-orange and blue-green, red-violet and yellow-green.

### TRIADS

Colors which are so positioned on our chart as to form equilateral triangles —i.e., (1) the three primaries, (2) the three secondaries, (3) the two trios of intermediates—are sometimes known as "triads." *Just as complementary colors form dull grayish hues when intermixed, so do triads.* (This should be obvious, for if you mix together the triad red, yellow, and blue, it is the same as if you mixed red and green—for what is green but a combination of yellow and blue?) It naturally follows that *if you intermix a lot of miscellaneous colors from different parts of the circle the resultant is almost sure to be a dull gray or brown—sometimes a gray-green.* (The reader can learn a valuable lesson from this simple fact. If he wishes any passage in a painting to be colorful, he must render it with fairly large areas of a few intense colors; the more hues he intermixes, or applies in such small dots that the eye automatically intermixes them, the more neutral his passage will appear.)

### A STRANGE PARADOX

One of the most amazing and fascinating things about color is this: We have seen that complementary colors, in mixture, tend to annihilate each other. Contrarily, *when placed side by side each intensifies the other.* Test this for yourself. If you wish to make an area of orange look all the brighter, surround it with an area of complementary blue; the blue through contrast will definitely increase the apparent brightness of the orange. Also, the blue in turn will seem brighter because of the orange.

Here is a practical application: If you are picturing a building bathed in the yellows and oranges of sunlight, and you wish to make it look still more sunny, you can advantageously use, adjacent to or surrounding these warm colors, cooler colors such as blue, blue-violet, and blue-green, thus creating (through what is known as "simultaneous contrast") an illusion of brighter light. One reason why artists employ so many blue and purple shadows is that they have learned that through complementary contrast they can make their sunny areas more brilliant in effect.

*63*

*Carl Gaertner:* THE SWAMP RECLAIMS   *This subtle color
scheme is dominated by browns with analogous rusty tones. These
analogous colors are, in turn, played off against
the complementary bluish tones of the snow.*

When it comes to everyday color mixture, you will discover the value of your chart again and again. As a single example, let us suppose that you have mixed red-violet on your palette and that it is a little too bright for your purpose. You know from your chart—which you should endeavor to memorize, keeping it before you until you do—that by adding yellow-green to your red-violet you will dull it. (You could also dull it through the addition of black or gray, but more pleasing colors are usually generated through mixing more colorful hues.)

### COLOR SCHEMES

In Chapter 6 we shall deal at some length with color schemes, another highly important consideration in which the color wheel can prove very helpful.

To give in advance a specific application, in one common type of color scheme the artist limits his palette so that the larger areas of his canvas are covered with analogous hues. Thus he is practically sure of harmony of color as all his hues are related. To gain the desired relief from monotony, however, he utilizes small areas of complementary colors. (In a Corot landscape we may find the canvas largely covered with grass and foliage masses of neutralized green. To bring relief to this green and enliven the whole, the artist effectively uses a small area of red—perhaps a cow or a boy's cap or coat.)

### A SUCCESSFUL SCHEME

Study many paintings and you will discover that, in these analogous schemes with complementary accents, the artist often selects for the larger areas of any given painting the analogous colors which are found in approximately one-third or one-quarter of the circumference of our color wheel. He then goes to the opposite side of the wheel for complementary colors to be used in relatively small areas only. (Maxfield Parrish has often given us quite brilliant instances of this type of scheme by covering large areas—sky, sea, trees—with blues, blue-greens, and blue-violets, then throwing strong sunny yellow and orange hues on a smaller area such as a figure, a tree trunk, a rock, a fountain, or a sail, spotlighting it, as it were.)

Although comparatively small complementary areas can thus be effective, *the employment of anything like equal areas of two full-strength complementary colors can be highly dangerous;* it often creates a chromatic clash. In other words, it is generally best not to paint large adjoining or adjacent areas with opposite or competing colors of any great brilliancy unless you are intentionally working for a dazzling, unrestful effect. Usually, when opposites are conspicuously employed one or the other should dominate either in area or hue. To illustrate, if a painting were to be made with roughly one-half of its area bright red (a red barn, perhaps) and one-half of its area bright green (the foliage around the barn) there would be no dominant hue. We would have, instead, an unpleasant clash of opposites, a fighting for supremacy. To prevent such a chromatic battle, the green could be dulled, leaving the red to dominate, or vice versa. Or the areas might be adjusted in size so that one or the other color would dominate through mere bulk.

### NEUTRALIZED COLORS

Of course *very few painters regularly use their more brilliant colors in large areas and full strength*—results would be too garish. And the less brilliant one's colors are in any given painting, the less the danger of obtaining a chromatically inharmonious result. If, for instance, a little red (or gray) is mixed into almost all of the greens, and a little green (or gray) into almost all of the reds, this common factor will tend to bring these naturally opposing colors into closer harmony. Other complementary pairs could be similarly treated. (Many colors, as purchased, have already been neutralized in one way or another by the manufacturer.)

In order to create harmony, *artists frequently use complementary colors to neutralize the shade or shadow side of an object.* If one is painting a blue bowl, a certain amount of complementary orange can often be employed to advantage in the shady side. A yellow bowl might have some violet worked into the shade areas, and so on. Use restraint, however; shade and shadow areas should never be too prominent.

### TIMIDITY

Don't neutralize *everything.* It is perhaps better, particulary at first, to risk garishness or stridency through the use of overbright colors than to risk monotony or insipidity through an attempt to harmonize everything.

*Exercise 14: Some color considerations*
Why not make some little sketches, or paint experimental areas, to illustrate the above points? And you might also like to hunt for examples—either actual paintings or reproductions in color.

### NO FOOLPROOF KEY TO HARMONY

This brings us to a most important fact. *No one, no matter how expert, can give you rules or a system which will guarantee that you will always obtain successful color schemes in your paintings*—or anywhere else for that matter. Many have tried, and some offer charts, gadgets, or systems which they claim or imply will ensure successful schemes. Don't be fooled by such claims or implications. I am by no means condemning all such charts, gadgets or systems, for some of them can be very useful up to a point—and well worth their price. But they will take you only so far.

There are two outstanding reasons why no infallible rules for color harmony can be offered: (1) *Colors which are harmonious when employed in areas of a certain size may be inharmonious if used in areas of a different size.* (2) *Colors which prove pleasing in some arrangements may clash or at least prove ineffective in other arrangements.*

*Exercise 15: Experiments in area*
We've already briefly discussed this first point but let's take a closer look. Select some colored sheets of paper—clippings from colorful booklet covers will do. From these, pick the most inharmonious pair of colors you can find. Then, with your scissors, snip out areas of these same colors varying in size and pair them up. Study each pair by itself. Just as a small area of bright red usually looks effective placed next to a large area of bright green, so one of your small clippings will quite possibly prove pleasing in combination with a larger clipping of the other color. *Artists often bring a clashing combination of two or more colors into harmonious relationship by the mere expedient of changing the areas in size.* Designers of millinery, dresses, rugs, etc., have long since learned the importance of thus restraining certain colors as to area, while expanding others. Rules can be of little help here; the trained eye is the best guide.

*Exercise 16: An area phenomenon*

In order to test still further the importance of color areas, paint, side by side, each three or four inches in extent, an area of bright red and a like area of bright green. Here you have the typical and very lively—and not too harmonious—complementary color combination repeatedly mentioned, each color heightening the other through contrast. Now, using the very same red and green colors, stripe a third area of similar size with alternating red and green stripes just as narrow as you can make them with your finest brush. (Try not to allow the two colors to intermix or overlap.) Next, place these various areas, plain and striped, eight or ten feet away. At this distance the first pair of colors—the first two squares—will still look bright. The narrow stripes, however, will run together, merged by the eye into a somewhat neutral tone, much as though the paints themselves were blended together. This gives us definite proof that *color area in your paintings has much to do with color appearances.*

Fine brush marks (lines, dashes, dots) of even the brightest colors will be optically blended when viewed from a normal distance, opposing colors fading away amazingly. *For this reason, don't, when painting your pictures, intermingle a lot of little brush marks of bright complementary hues and expect them to exhibit chromatic brilliancy.* If you juxtapose brush marks of analogous colors you will often create lively, scintillating effects. In fact, the "pointillistic" method of the impressionists was based on this use of myriad small spots of varying hue—generally analogous but sometimes complementary—placed in close proximity.

(Incidentally, a main reason why it is next to impossible to print satisfactory color reproductions of some paintings is that areas which, in the original, are large enough to be chromatically effective are so greatly reduced in reproduction that, like the stripes mentioned above, they lose their power. Illustrators have learned that when painting for reduction it is necessary to keep color areas large and simple.)

SUMMARY

Three facts which stand out from all of this discussion are: (1) large areas of opposite colors, juxtaposed, tend to intensify each other; (2) contrarily, myriad small areas of opposite colors, similarly juxtaposed, are blended by the eye into neutral tone, each color tending to annihilate its opposite; and (3) opposite colors when mixed together also tend to neutralize or annihilate each other.

HOW GOOD ARE you at judging colors, matching them one against another? If I were to lay before you a dozen or more squares or circles of colored paper, each an inch or so in size, could you pick out by eye (without changing their relative positions) two or more which might actually be absolutely identical in hue? Could you do this no matter what the hue of their background, and regardless of their arrangement on this background? If so, you are exceptional. Few people can correctly judge colors in all arrangements; nature gives us many optical illusions.

*Exercise 17: Color arrangement*

But test the thing for yourself. Place side by side two fairly large sheets of paper (at least five or six inches square), one of them light yellow and the other of dark but intense blue. On these, lay two small squares (or other convenient shapes) of bright green paper. So arranged, the green against the dark blue will seem lighter than before and slightly yellowish, while the green against the light yellow will appear darker and slightly blue-green. (Lay transparent tissue paper over the whole and the contrast will be even more pronounced; it sometimes is hard to believe that the two green squares are actually of identical hue.) Not only will the two small green areas thus differ in apparent value and hue, but the yellow, contrasted with the green and blue, may appear slightly towards orange and the blue, contrasted with the yellow and green, a bit purple. In short, a few such experiments will demonstrate clearly that *colors are influenced in hue by adjacent colors, each tinting its neighbor with its own complement.*

The experimenter, using papers of other colors (or areas of paint, if he prefers) will also learn that *dark hues on a dark ground which is not complementary will appear weaker than on one which is; light colors on a light ground which is not complementary will seem weaker than on a complementary ground; a bright color against a dull color of the same hue will further deaden the dull color; when a bright color is used against a dull color the contrast will be strongest when the latter is complementary; light colors on light grounds (not complementary) can be greatly strengthened if bounded by narrow bands of black or complementary colors; and dark colors on dark grounds (not complementary) can be strengthened if similarly bounded by white or light colors.*

Just how does all of this affect the painter when he goes forth to interpret nature's hues? Not much, actually. But because he has learned how tricky nature can be, he realizes the truth of our claim on an earlier page that any rules of color harmony—any hope of learning to paint by rote—is out of the question. Also, he will not be surprised by the way in which some of his colors will seem to vary in appearance under different conditions. He will understand that not only do colors vary according to their location in relation to other colors, but, as we saw previously, they also vary according to area. We might sum this up by saying that *colors are not always what they seem to be.* A given color in one size and placing may look amazingly different from the identical hue in another size and placing. This is true both in nature and in painting.

COLOR ACTIVITY

Regardless of size or arrangement, areas of color differ greatly in their affective and attentive value. Some colors can best be described as active, lively, restless, insistent, positive, bold, expanding, or advancing; others seem passive, negative, subdued, timid, submissive, reserved, contracting, or retreating. Some suggest warmth and others coolness; some impress us as heavy and inert and others as light and animated. The student should cultivate the habit of sizing up different colors which he sees about him,

*70*

noting their characteristics and his reactions to them. When it comes to painting, the discrimination which this practice develops will help him to choose those colors best fitted to his mood and purpose, a matter of great importance.

### WARM AND COOL COLORS

Of these various characteristics, some seem particularly significant or are sufficiently tangible to be understood easily and put to practical use. That certain colors seem warm and others cool is a thing of which advantage can often be taken. Hues of the red, orange, and yellow group are the ones considered warm; they suggest flame, blood and sunshine, and are especially appropriate when bright, stimulating effects are sought. Hues which are blue, or analogous to blue, are thought of as cool; they bring to mind cool water and ice and the sky of winter and are at their best (there are exceptions of course) for purposes requiring restraint and subordination.

### ADVANCING AND RETREATING COLORS

Cool colors also suggest distance or expansion and are therefore called "retreating" colors, while warm colors, contrarily, are classed as "advancing." If we wish to paint distance or make areas seem spacious we therefore give preference to cool colors; in the foreground, or where we wish attention concentrated, we use warm ones. As warm colors generally are associated with light, so cool colors suggest shadow, another important fact that we apply when painting.

Of the various advancing colors, red and orange are considered to have the greatest force. Advertisers use them, particularly the former, as a means of gaining maximum attention. The artist employs them when he wishes to emphasize particularly a portion of his subject. Yellow is an exceptionally strong color under some conditions but usually has less power than red and orange. It carries well and has compelling force against dark or complementary backgrounds, or if bordered or accented with dark, but is relatively weak if contrasted with light tints or white. (Here we are again reminded of the importance of color arrangement.)

Retreating colors, though carrying well as dark spots, often show weakness of hue if viewed from a distance. Greens and violets stand at the halfway point between heat and cold, as they contain both warm and cool colors, and so vary proportionately in their abilities to advance or recede. Yellow-greens, and violets leaning strongly towards red, tend to advance and have considerable power to attract; blue-greens and blue-violets tend to recede, and have less compelling force.

The carrying or attractive power of colors depends not alone on hue, but also on value and intensity. A gray-red, for example, though it may attract as a dark spot, will have little force compared with the same red when not neutralized. This will be plainly evident if slips of paper of these colors are placed across the room.

We have seen that the activity of colors depends to no small extent on background. Distance, too, plays an important part in color strength. If one looks down a long city street with brick buildings on either hand one will generally observe that the reds of the brickwork appear more and more dull or indistinct as they go into the distance, particularly if the atmosphere is a bit hazy; a blue or purplish hue will gradually take the place of the red as extreme distance is approached. In other words, *warm tones usually appear cooler in proportion to their distance from the eye.* To some extent this is true of all colors. Cool colors do not always seem to retreat, by the way; certain vivid hues, viewed near-by, appear particularly vigorous and emphatic, especially if against a complementary background. I recently noticed, near at hand, a bright blue automobile which, contrasted with brown and red buildings, seemed extremely conspicuous. As it drove into the distance, its color softened progressively.

As a practical application of advancing and receding hues, when painting landscapes or marines it is customarily well to use your brightest colors in the foreground, and duller and duller colors as you work into the distance. This is not only because bright colors are more advancing than dull colors, but it is also in line with the basic rule that all hues in nature, whether dull or bright, tend to be veiled in mist and atmospheric impurities in proportion to their distance from the spectator.

*Exercise 18: Further color experiments*
What we have offered here is by no means expected to clarify the entire many-faceted subject of color. It is included mainly to show what a complex thing color is, and to emphasize the need for serious study and experimentation on the part of the earnest student. Read the previous text once more and perform such exercises as occur to you. But don't hope to master the whole thing at one time!

*John Wells James:* SUMMER BOUQUET *This very delicate composition is unified by blue, the color which acts as an underlying element in the entire painting. Blue appears in the tablecloth, in the background, shadows, green foliage, and violet tone of the flowers. Its complement appears in the orange flowers.*

There's one encouraging thing: one can even paint successfully (and many artists do) with little knowledge of the reasons behind such matters as we have been discussing. And many so-called "experts" on color can't paint at all! Don't feel, in other words, that you must devote days and days to color study before trying your hand at actual representational painting. Pitch in and paint. But observe color and think about it often. Gradually your color knowledge will grow.

# Chapter 6

# COLOR SCHEMES

PERHAPS WE ARE a bit premature in offering the paragraphs below, for you may feel that you will have enough to worry about in making your first paintings without endeavoring to obtain harmonious color effects. So turn at once to Chapter 7 if you feel so inclined. Yet these present suggestions seem so fitting a corollary to what we have already said that we can think of no more logical time to present them. At least they may serve to inspire the beginning painter to observe color more keenly and to think more often along color lines.

### THERE ARE NO RULES

From our foregoing discussions—and from your experiments—we hope that you are by now convinced that there can be no rules to guarantee the artist a successful color scheme for a painting. You have learned that such a scheme depends not alone on the *selection* of hues which in themselves are harmonious, but also on the relative *size* of the areas in which they are used, as well as the *arrangement* of these areas.

If no teacher can tell you precisely how to obtain good color schemes —and no teacher can—possibly you have the hope that nature will prove a safe guide. If so, you may be somewhat disappointed. Nature, to be sure, gives you many beautiful color schemes to serve as an inspiration and, to some extent, as a guide. Yet if you try to copy one by one, as precisely as you can, the hues which nature sets before you so attractively, you will quite possibly produce either discords of hue, or, more likely, schemes so dull and commonplace as to prove uninteresting. This is partly because nature's colors are *living* colors (perhaps bathed in brilliant light, or modified by mist, smoke, and the like) while yours are merely pigments, so that no matter how accurately you think you are matching each one of nature's hues as you paint, your final result is almost certain to lack much of the luminosity, the vibration, the subtle nuances, the chromatic richness, and unity of the model before you. (Eventually you will learn to go after big *impressions* of natural color, not a matching of each hue.)

If paintings by the novice fail in any one general chromatic respect, it is that they are so worked over, or done with so timid a brush, that they become lifeless and static—too muddy and gray. Or, because the artist senses this fault and endeavors to rectify or avoid it as he works, perhaps by applying pure color just as it comes from the tube, his results may grow too garish and extravagant, one hue clashing with another. Either of these extreme conditions should be avoided.

Yet color is obviously of great importance. An otherwise poor painting which is superior in color often wins acclaim while an otherwise good painting, poor in color, usually ranks as a failure. Some of the best paintings, regardless of size, subject matter, or technical handling, appeal to us largely for their color excellence—their esthetically satisfying choice and disposition of hues. Often such colors are close to nature—but often not—and this doesn't seem to matter so long as the spectator finds the result pleasing to his eye.

But, if there are no man-made rules, and if nature is not an infallible guide, how is the painter to master color so as to produce satisfactory schemes? That is not easy to answer. Some beginners seldom have trouble with color; they are born with a color sense that others can acquire only after long study, if at all. Most beginners gain mastery gradually, mainly through trial and error.

One way is to "borrow" proven schemes from the paintings of others; there is nothing wrong in this provided you employ them naturally instead of trying to force them into use. You can also adapt schemes from such things as colored prints, rugs, wallpapers, upholstery, and drapery materials. The student is wise who makes notes of attractive color schemes everywhere he sees them, doing quick color sketches from paintings in the museums and galleries, clipping color reproductions from magazines, experimenting with his paints in an endeavor to find hues which go well together. Often a color scheme, borrowed from nature, can later be adapted to different subject matter, also from nature. A group of flowers, for instance, might provide the color scheme for an entire landscape painting. In short, the artist considers it his right to rearrange or otherwise alter nature's colorings if it suits his purpose or fancy.

### ONE COLOR WITH WHITE, GRAY, OR BLACK

The simplest scheme makes use of a single color of only one value and intensity in conjunction with white, gray, or black (and, sometimes, with silver or gold). Such a scheme is seldom used by the painter; it is more commonly found in decoration or design. (A typical illustration is the booklet printed with black ink on white paper, with initials or decorations of one tone of some other hue.)

### THE MONOCHROMATIC SCHEME

The simplest scheme which the painter is likely to employ is an extension of the above; it consists of any desired values and intensities of a single hue, used with or without white, gray, or black. A good illustration would be a painting done on white paper or canvas with but one color—burnt umber, for example—the values perhaps ranging from light tints to dark shades. (Such variations are sometimes referred to as "self-tones.") As only one color is used (hence the term "monochromatic"), there is no chance for an inharmonious color result. That monochromatic schemes can be effective is proved by the fact that all but colored photographs are in monochrome—usually black or brown.

### THE MODIFIED MONOCHROMATIC SCHEME

Seldom is the painter satisfied with a strictly monochromatic treatment. In order to gain slightly more variety he often adds subtle suggestions of other colors, thus obtaining by economical means an impression of a satisfying opulence of hue. Occasionally, small touches of bright colors are used in painting which otherwise is monochromatic. For example, most of the

77

canvas might be covered with varying tones of gray-blue (as in a night scene), small accents being added of complementary orange (lights in the windows, perhaps). In a further extension of this type of scheme, the effect would be generally monochromatic, but the dominant hue would be subtly supported by suggestions of analogous hues, the whole then being intensified through the use of small (possibly bright) complementary accents.

### ANALOGOUS SCHEMES

Inasmuch as strictly monochromatic schemes are rare in the work of the painter, his main interest will be in various types of more colorful schemes. The simplest of these is the analogous or related scheme already discussed in connection with our color wheel (Figure 20). It will be recalled that this scheme is made up of colors which are adjoining or adjacent in the spectrum, and hence on the color wheel. Orange, yellow and yellow-green, for example, form an analogous scheme for they all contain the common factor, yellow.

Let me repeat that it is well to keep such a color wheel at hand, for it shows at a glance what color groups are analogous. If we start with yellow (we might similarly begin with red or blue) we note that yellow-orange and yellow-green, consisting largely of yellow, are particularly close in relationship. These three form a "close" analogy, and so are almost certain to be harmonious. If we reach out to include orange and green, each of which contains some yellow, this entire five-hue group is also analogous and usually a safe combination. We can also often include red-orange and blue-green with reasonable safety (for each possesses a slight yellow content). The more of the circle we include, however, the more varied the elements which must be harmonized, so typical analogous schemes seldom take in more than a third of the circle, centering around one of the primary colors, red, yellow, and blue. Such schemes are among the safest and surest at the artist's command.

In other words, if you want to obtain harmonious color, limit yourself to a few hues showing a clear indication of mutual relationship. We should perhaps warn you, however, that even this is no absolute guarantee of success. I recently noticed a florist's delivery truck of pale violet parked beside a huge sun-bathed trailer truck of red-orange. The common factor of red was not enough to relate the two hues pleasingly; the delicate violet was entirely out of keeping with the vigor of the red-orange. But this is exceptional.

### WITH DOMINANT HUE

The very unification or close harmony which makes analogous schemes pleasing can at times make them monotonous. To convert them into something more interesting, it is often well to place emphasis on some one hue of an analogous group—in other words, to make this hue dominant. Always remember that a hue can be made to dominate because of its large area, its dark value (against lighter hues), its light value (against darker hues), or its intensity.

### WITH COMPLEMENTARY ACCENTS

As we saw in Chapter 4, many of the most successful analogous schemes are enlivened by the introduction of rather small but sometimes intense complementary accents. Such accents, particularly if brilliant, often have a power out of all proportion to their size. A single touch of color complementary to the dominant hue of an analogous scheme can give surprising life to the whole.

### COMPLEMENTARY SCHEMES

It is but a step from this use of complementary accents to completely complementary schemes, sometimes known as "harmonies of contrast." Under this heading we can include any pleasing schemes which conspicuously introduce opposite colors. The majority of color schemes used in paintings are to some extent contrasting, the contrast generally being developed through the use of complements.

Despite the fact that colors which we term complements are wholly unlike in most respects, it should always be remembered that a definite relationship nevertheless exists between them. Green and red, for instance, while in most respects as unlike as any two colors could possibly be, are nevertheless subtly related, as the word "complement" implies. When properly handled, complements can result in some of our most pleasing color harmonies of analogy. Some of the finest paintings, chromatically, contain *all* the leading colors in balanced pairs. Nature, too, is profuse with complementary schemes.

We must learn to control our contrasts, however, or we may get, instead of harmony, chaos. Generally speaking, *never base a color scheme on complementary colors in equal areas and full strength*. A dress made of alternating wide stripes of intense orange and blue would compel attention, but it could scarcely be called harmonious! But we have previously seen that we can employ complements to advantage in unequal areas or intensities. We know that a large red area and a small green area often look well together, as does a brilliant red area contrasted with a dull green area. And vice versa.

*Exercise 19: After-images*
To interrupt for a minute, did you ever play around with after-images? They are fascinating! They prove, among other things, the truth of what we have just said about complements being subtly related.

But test them for yourself; it will take but a second. Place (or paint) a small area of bright green—an inch will do—in the middle of a sheet of white paper (or canvas). Light it well. Then stare at it fixedly for half a minute. Now shift the eye quickly to the center of another white sheet. Almost at once—wait for it—a light pinkish "ghost" will appear, stay for a few seconds and then gradually fade away. That ghost is a pale tint of the true complement of that particular green. Try other colors and find this ghost of the complement of each. You can even stare at several adjacent spots of different color simultaneously, and then see on another sheet the ghost complements of all of them.

In performing such an experiment, by the way, you will doubtless be struck by an interesting phenomenon. As you stare fixedly at an area of any given color you will soon note that by gradual degrees it grows duller and duller before your very eyes. It is being neutralized (as the eye temporarily becomes tired) by its own complement! Perhaps as you stare you can see this complementary tint "bleeding" along the edges of the color area. By shifting your glance, you can transfer it to another paper.

### NEAR AND SPLIT COMPLEMENTS

Returning to our main thought, in harmonies of a complementary nature, the eye does not demand that *exact* complements be used. This would be difficult, even if desirable. Fortunately, complements which are only approximate or "near" seem more pleasing, many times, than those which are absolute. The term "near complements" is self-explanatory; violet is the true complement of yellow, while blue-violet and red-violet are both near complements of yellow. We sometimes speak of these in their relationship, one to the other, as "split" complements, as they are split or separated by the true complement, violet.

### TRIADS

If we base a color scheme on a color and its split complements, or on hues mixed from them, we can obtain a fairly wide range of hues, but none of them can be brighter than the color itself and the two split complements in their full intensity. Sometimes such a range proves too limited, so in place of these split complements, which are closely related to the complement itself, we use other split complements, each a step further removed.

In the twelve-color wheel (Figure 20), if yellow should be taken as a hue to dominate a color scheme, and the split complements red-violet and blue-violet (alone or in mixture) should prove too inadequate to hold their own, red and blue might be substituted, giving us a "triad" harmony. Yet here we are of course in a danger zone, for although some mixtures obtained from triads can be very rich and beautiful (we have seen again and again that practically all colors can be mixed from the triad composed of red, yellow, and blue), other mixtures can be far from harmonious as each primary strives to dominate the other two. To get effective results, therefore, one hue of the triad is usually selected to dominate the scheme, and the other two are mixed together, or with the first, or with white or black or some other color so as to render them less potent.

One of the most certain ways of preventing rivalry among the basic colors of a triad is to select one of the three to dominate, and then to "veil" or neutralize the other two with it. This veiling can be done through admixture or by scumbling—see pages 153 and 154.

### A PLAY-SAFE METHOD

For the beginner, incidentally, there is a "play-safe" type of harmony which gives him reasonably satisfactory chromatic balance simply and quickly; he merely distributes some of each of his leading hues all over the canvas, blending a bit of "this" into a bit of "that" throughout the whole, thus weaving a sort of all-over pattern of color. Thus no one color is vigorous enough in hue, intensity or area to clash with any other.

### IT'S VERY COMPLICATED

Don't expect to grasp from this all-too-brief (yet undoubtedly confusing) printed word more than a vague notion of the intricacies of color harmony. Some painters have concentrated on it for a lifetime, and entire books have been devoted to it. May I stress again that my main purpose is merely to get you thinking about color, so as to develop as you go along a more critical color sense, plus an ever-increasing facility in harmonizing the various hues at your command.

*Exercise 20: Color schemes*
Make some small color sketches to illustrate the types of schemes discussed above, or hunt up pictorial illustrations of each in books or magazines.

*Helen Wolf:* GREEN APPLES   *The color scheme in this bold
still life painting is dominated by warm yellows and oranges.
A certain zest is given to the painting by the cool accents
of blue and green. This sharp contrast of complementary colors
is softened by the panel of neutral gray in the background. Alfred
Khouri Collection, Norfolk Museum of Arts and Sciences.*

# Chapter 7
## SIMPLE
## LESSONS FROM
## STILL LIFE

IT APPEARS THAT a majority of beginners—at least this is true of amateurs —are primarily interested in the painting of landscapes and other out-of-door subjects. If you are one of these and impatient to get at your first work in the open, you may turn immediately to Chapter 11. There are, however, one or two highly important technical matters not yet dealt with which you could profitably consider at this point by way of further preparation for all of your future work, whether indoors or out. For example, when it comes to painting pictures, in what directions will you make your brush (or knife) strokes? Second, how will you represent surfaces according to whether they are in light, shade or shadow? Third, how will you indicate the surfaces and textures of objects so as to make them look flat or rounded, dull or shiny, rough or smooth?

I shall answer these queries in a somewhat roundabout manner, starting with the definite statement that there is no way in which one can get to understand some of the basic appearances in nature, and at the same time gain skill in their pictorial interpretation, as quickly and as well as through the careful observation and representation of the simplest and most easily comprehended subjects which we can find—namely, geometric solids such as the sphere, cone, cube, and prism, or the almost-as-simple still-life objects based upon these solids: things like little boxes and dishes.

Admittedly it may not sound very inspiring to start one's painting by doing an egg, a tennis ball or a cracker box, but after years of teaching painting and drawing, I'm willing to wager that a few hours—or, better yet, a few days—of painting from these apparently inconsequential little things can set you ahead further than anything else you could possibly do. A sufficient amount of such practice can overcome almost every weakness that you have.

Of course the importance of such practice lies in the fact that everything which we see in nature—even the most complex of subjects—follows the same natural laws of appearance that are so easily discovered by observing and painting these simple objects—objects so small and so elementary that we may work from them with the greatest of ease, and at our leisure. They won't move, or change in shape or color.

**FORM**

Let us consider form or proportion, for example. If you learn to draw a tennis ball or an egg, that automatically teaches you much about drawing the basic shape of a dome, which is, after all, nothing but a hemisphere. If you master the small cylinder, placed both vertically and horizontally, you will grasp the principle of the appearance of the cylindrical water tank, the log, or tree trunk, the hut. The end of the cylinder is of course a circle. If you master the delineation of the circle as viewed from every angle you should have little difficulty drawing wheels, hoops, and a thousand other things. The cube or square prism teaches you how to draw the house or

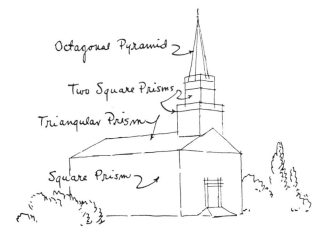

*Figure 21*
CONSTRUCTION *Much subject matter is based in general form on such geometric solids as the sphere and cube.*

*Leon Kroll:* TWO YOUNG GIRLS  *This painter is noted for the
sculptural quality of his figures, a strong feeling of geometry
which you can easily see in this painting. Notice how the
arms, necks, and even fingers are modeled like cylinders. The
heads are modeled like eggs and the vertical folds of the
dresses like cylinders. This modeling clearly defines
the architectural planes of the background.
Cone Collection, Baltimore Museum of Art*

barn, while the triangular prism gives you an understanding of its roof. If we analyze the church, Figure 21, we discover that, from the ground up, its basic elements are a square prism and a triangular prism, while its spire consists merely of two square prisms surmounted by an octagonal pyramid.

"But," you say, "I want to paint trees and mountains and ships, things far removed from these simple solids. Why waste my time on them?" While it's true, of course, that at first glance subject matter seldom follows these elementary geometric forms precisely (if we except things like some buildings and furniture), it is nevertheless true that even the most complex subject is often more closely related to such simple forms than we think. A tree, for example, is not unlike a sphere (or a group of spheres); see Figure 22, A and B. Or, a tree may recall a cone—see C. Speaking of trees, the stump of a tree is often cylindrical in form (D), or it may flare at the bottom in a somewhat cone-like manner (E). A complex form such as a sofa or a locomotive is often a combination of several basic shapes, but, by way of simplicity, we can think of it as "frozen into a block of ice"—see F. We can easily imagine many a complex subject thus related to a simple solid; if we first draw that solid, this will help us to get the object correct in proportion and perspective.

*Figure 22*
SIMPLIFYING FORM *Learn to draw simple things well and more complex things will cause little if any trouble.*

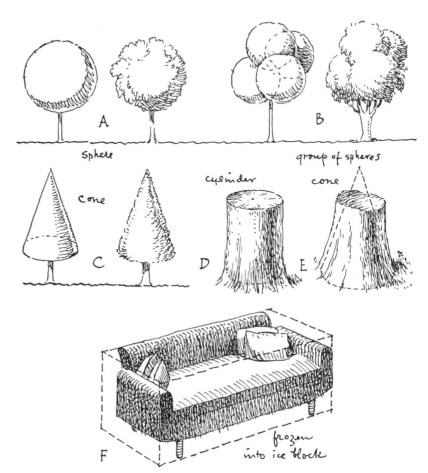

So much for the *form* or *proportion* of an object, which, after all, is not our main problem in this book. Now let's think a bit about the subject of *values*, which definitely is our problem. One advantage offered by the plain geometric solids, such as the wooden or plaster models sometimes used in schools, is that they are plain white. In other words, they have no local values other than white. Any variety of tone which they possess, therefore, results from light, shade, and shadow. Take a sphere, for example. That part of it turned most directly towards the light—the window, perhaps—will be the lightest (A, Figure 23). As the surface curves gradually away

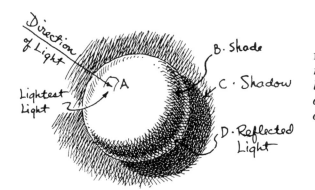

*Figure 23*

LIGHTING *Many of nature's effects depend largely on the kind, amount, and direction of illumination.*

from this point, it will receive less and less light, so will appear darker and darker. Those visible areas turned away the farthest from the light source will look quite dark. Such areas (B, Figure 23) are the "shade" areas. (Webster defines the noun *shade* as "comparative obscurity owing to interception of rays of light; darkness.") More than likely the sphere will cast a shadow on the supporting surface or on some background behind it (C, Figure 23). For *shadow* Webster says, "obscurity within a space from which rays are cut off by an interposing body. Also, the image made by such an obscured space on a surface that cuts across it; as the *shadow* of a man." This latter meaning is the one common to art, *shade* customarily being *on* an object and *shadow* cast by the object.

### REFLECTED LIGHT

A supporting plane, a background or another object, incidentally, often throws some light back onto the underneath or most distant areas of an object—"reflected light," this is called. (D, Figure 23.)

*88*

This light, shade, and shadow appearance of the sphere is followed in general by any rounded object in nature: vegetables and fruit, the human head and body, the balloon or spherical tank, the boulder, the hill, the tree, even the cloud. Each such object has areas turned towards the light, and usually they appear the lightest of any areas and must be so painted. Areas which turn away receive progressively less and less light and so look darker and darker unless reflected light modifies them.

Like the sphere, the cube can give us other lessons of light, shade and shadow, as can every one of the simple solids mentioned. In painting a cube (or a barn, for that matter), the painter asks himself, "Which surface receives the most light?" knowing that in truly representational painting he must make this the lightest. Then he asks, "Which is number two, receiving a little less light? Which is number three?" These he paints with this lighting in mind.

Never forget this simple and valuable lesson. Whenever you start to paint, look for the sun (or other source of illumination) and then, in doing each detail, ask yourself "How strongly is it lighted; to what degree does it face the light?" Or, "To what degree is it turned away?" Then paint accordingly.

*Exercise 21: Painting light objects*
The only way in which you can gain full advantage from these simple objects, light in value, is to paint them. It would be well for you to paint a few of the basic solids such as the sphere, cube and cone. (These, inci-

*Figure 24A*
SPHERE, CONE, AND CUBE

dentally, were painted wholly with white and burnt umber.) If such models are not available, you can always find cracker boxes, paper bags, and other objects light in value, or you can make models from cardboard or paper, as shown below.

*Figure 24B*
**CARDBOARD BOX**

**WARNING**

In painting such light objects—and this will always be true regardless of your subject matter—don't get the shade and shadow tones too dark. Because of simultaneous contrast, the dark areas of light objects always look darker than they are. We all know, for example, that a light suit often shows wrinkles more plainly than a dark suit. Similarly, when painting light objects, we are often more aware of their shade and shadow areas than we are in the case of darker objects. We *know*, however, that dark objects *must* have shades and shadows darker than those of light objects; therefore they should be so painted.

There is, though, an exception to this general rule. It so happens that many dark objects are smooth and shiny. Like any shiny objects, they mirror an unusual amount of light. Some of the areas of reflection are highlights—pure white or nearly so. Others, while not so light, are nevertheless lighter than we might expect. And, because the surrounding areas are so dark, these lights often appear, through simultaneous contrast, lighter than they are. In other words, when painting shiny objects, whether light or dark, you never know quite what to expect in the way of values.

*90*

This is illustrated to some extent by the mug. The mug itself was white but the bands of glaze were practically black. While the little painting makes this reasonably clear, the artist nevertheless discovered as he worked that these bands did not appear as dark in relation to the adjoining white areas as would seem logical. In the shade areas near the handle there was, in fact, but little difference in value between white and black areas. (Incidentally, in painting these illustrations, many of the brush marks were made more conspicuous than necessary, in order to indicate their direction.)

*Exercise 22: Painting dark objects*
The best way to master such differences in value is to paint at this time a few dark objects, or, better yet, light objects having dark areas which, like the bands on the mug just mentioned, are partly in light and partly in shade.

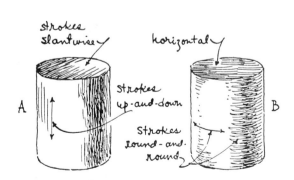

*Figure 24C*
DRINKING MUG

### BRUSH STROKE DIRECTION

These simple objects not only can teach you a lot about form and values, as we have just demonstrated, but they will also give you priceless lessons in answer to your thought, "In what direction shall I make my brush strokes?" Sometimes strokes are so entirely obliterated in one's finished work that their direction doesn't matter, but usually at least traces of direction are visible. Many artists therefore deliberately carry their strokes in the directions which will best suggest the form—especially the third dimensional appearance or "modeling"—of each object depicted. Take a cylinder, for example; the strokes on its cylindrical surfaces may very logically run up-and-down (A, Figure 25), or round-and-round (B, Figure 25). In the case of a cube, there is a greater choice of direction. Strokes on

*Figure 25*
BRUSHWORK *Brush strokes often take the directions which best depict the modeling of the forms represented.*

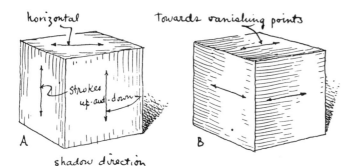

*Figure 26*
**BRUSHWORK** *Straight strokes are frequently best for flat surfaces and curved strokes for curved surfaces.*

the vertical surfaces might be painted vertically (A, Figure 26), or they might converge towards the vanishing points of the cube (B, Figure 26). Strokes on the horizontal surfaces—the top, in our example—might run horizontally, or, more likely, they might converge towards one of the vanishing points. Much the same thing would also be true of the top of a vertical cylinder (Figure 25). As to a sphere, the strokes might follow the curve of the surface in any of several directions as indicated by Figure 27. They might be concentrically arranged (a), they might radiate (b),

*Figure 27*
**BRUSHWORK** *As a rule, there is no one best direction for brush strokes, but several. Always work in the way which seems natural.*

or they might be more freely disposed (c). They might even slope so as to indicate to some extent the direction of the rays of light (d). Carrying the thought a bit further, in painting a book, the strokes might follow the direction of the edges of the leaves; on the "backbone" they might be rounded to suggest the curvature (e). The pattern on a bowl or vase might give a clue to successful brushwork direction. Turning to buildings out-of-doors, such things as the courses of shingles, bricks, and stones may suggest stroke directions, or the strokes may run vertically or converge towards the perspective vanishing points.

In the case of natural objects, nature herself often gives us the key. Fruits, vegetables and flowers often leave no doubt as to at least one logical approach, for it is natural for strokes to follow the direction of growth. A flower, for example, might be rendered with strokes radiating from the center (Figure 28, a), while a carrot might call for strokes round-and-round the form depicted (b). On a tree trunk or for tall grass,

92

strokes might sweep in an *upward* direction, thus suggesting growth (c), or, in order to emphasize natural action or direction of movement, they might curve *down* a waterfall (d) or *around* the curve of a wave.

### COLOR

But we are wandering from our subject: simple still-life objects and some of the lessons we can learn from them. We have now repeatedly seen that practice from such objects can help us to master form and values. As to color, they are equally good teachers. Obviously you must now choose colored objects; for our present purpose, the simpler they are, the better. Don't select things at first which have conspicuous pattern, but limit your choice to one or two objects such as simple fruit, or dishes not too complex in form or detail.

Any object which you choose for study should be viewed against an appropriate background; plain cardboard or cloth is good. Sometimes one sheet of cardboard is placed on the table top as an object rest, and another behind the object. Thus, other objects are shut out, which leaves you free to concentrate on the job at hand. Also, the lighting should be simple. Lights from several sources can create a disturbing perplexity of shade and shadow.

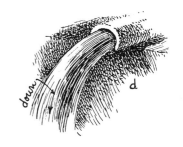

*Exercise 23: Painting colored objects*
Having selected an object or two and placed them where you can concentrate on them alone, ask yourself a lot of questions to make your observation more acute. In doing this, you are starting a procedure which you will continue, consciously or subconsciously, as long as you remain a painter.

I might add, parenthetically, that one of the greatest pleasures which the painter gets from his work all through life results from the fact that the more observant he becomes, the more he is aware of, and appreciative of, the shapes of things, the colors of things, the textures of things. In short, as his perception increases, the whole world becomes a source of ever new delights.

*Figure 28*
**BRUSHWORK** *Here are additional suggestions for stroke directions. Some painters prefer a very free use of strokes, disregarding nature's hints. The choice is yours.*

So you will start this course in observation by asking yourself, not only before you paint but as you proceed, questions like these: What is the shape of this object? What is its color? Is it light or dark in value? Is it lighted from above? From one side? Is the light bright? Is the light white (normal) or colored? Where does it hit most directly? Is that area the lightest on the object? Where is the darkest area? Does the vertical background look lighter or darker than the horizontal support? Are these background tones lighter or darker than the object? Does the object stand out distinctly against every part of the background? Do some parts stand out more distinctly than others? In other words, do some of the edges of the object look sharp and others soft? Are the shadows of the object uniform or graded? How dark do the shadows look in relation to the object? Where is the darkest area of shadow? The lightest? Are the edges of the shadow sharp or soft? What are the relative values of the shade areas? Is the object shiny, dull, smooth, rough? Is it heavy, light, yielding or unyielding?

Do such questions sound a bit silly? If you wish to become a painter, they aren't, because you can never paint things well unless you overcome any false notions as to their appearance and concentrate on observing as analytically as you can how they truly look. Learning to see—which means to see comprehendingly, to see with the mind as well as with the eye—has been called the most important step in representational painting, and it most certainly is!

Having studied your object, sketch it, set your palette with appropriate hues, and sail in! It is usually best, at this stage at least, to build up the whole thing gradually. Get some tone on everything as soon as you can; then add a bit more here and a bit more there, keeping the whole thing coming. Rest your eye now and then; nothing is more important, especially whenever you reach a point where you scarcely know what to do next. Keep your technique inconspicuous—suppress your individual brush strokes unless you truly need to emphasize some of them in order to interpret the subject successfully. Where your color looks the brightest, make it so. Where edges look sharp, paint them sharp. If anything, keep your painting even more simple than the subject. A common fault of the student is to over-emphasize tiny details, especially in the shade and shadow areas. Try always to suggest the "modeling" of the subject matter, bringing the nearer surfaces forward in effect as you carry the further surfaces back. Reflect your painting in a mirror from time to time so as to see it in reverse. Does it look convincing?

*94*

To summarize, you can gain great profit by working in this way for a while from the simplest of subject matter. Set yourself a definite course, trying something different every time you paint. Soon you will wish to combine several objects. In doing this, choose contrasting objects, so as to study one in relation to another. Contrast a square object with a round object, a light object with a dark object, a colorful object with a neutral object, a shiny object with a dull object. The paintings done at this time may not look like much, but you should work conscientiously, remembering that the lessons you learn from these small, simple, easily understood objects can be applied again and again as you turn to larger or more complex subject matter. Chapter 9 demonstrates pictorially this step-by-step process.

*John F. Carlson:* QUIET GROVES *Notice the way in which the painter suggests the textures of the bark, leaves, and snow. He combined bristle brushes and palette knives to achieve textural effects. Courtesy, Grand Central Art Galleries.*

WE CAN SCARCELY emphasize too often the fact that there are four outstanding appearance qualities or characteristics which every object reveals
to the eye, and with which the painter must be fully familiar, for it is
his job to represent all four on his canvas.

First, an object has its physical mass—its size and shape—and the
artist must know how to draw convincingly the proportions of this mass
as they appear, subject to the laws of perspective. (That is not, however,
a main concern of this book, for we assume that the reader can already
draw reasonably well.)

Second, an object has its values of light and dark. Some of these are
innate tones, dependent on the materials of which the object is fabricated
or with which it is decorated. (A pitcher may be of white clay with a black
band of glaze; the white and black are innate values.) Other values result
from the light which falls on an object; this light—which may be
either natural or artificial—creates areas of light, shade and shadow.

Third, an object has its colors. Colors, like values, may be innate (such
as the red clay of a brick or the green of a leaf) or they may be caused by
colored light thrown onto the subject. Occasionally both values and colors
are caused by some luminous quality of an object—the object may be a
lighted lamp or something fluorescent or phosphorescent, for example.

*Thomas Yerxa:* EMPTY PARKING LOT *The texture of the moldering walls is rendered very effectively with broken color and paint which is applied with an almost dry-brush technique. This rough texture contrasts with the soft atmospheric gradation of the sky. Collection, Mr. and Mrs. Nathaniel Jacobson.*

Fourth—and the subject of our present discussion—an object has its visible surface textures: it is rough or smooth, dull or shiny. Cloth, wood, human flesh, fur, plaster, glass, brass—everything which we see—has its own texture, often so characteristic that we can identify the object by texture alone. (Speaking of cloth, black felt, black velvet, and black brocade look very different in texture—to pick an example at random.)

It is almost as important to be able to indicate these textures well as it is to represent forms, values, and colors. The beginner, however, is sometimes slow in recognizing this; hence the emphasis which we give the subject at this time. Not that each of these four qualities must be indicated separately; actually we usually represent them in one and the same operation. As we paint, we work over every detail on our canvas until it looks right in all four respects: in shape, in tone, in color, in texture.

As mentioned in the previous chapter, when you are about to paint any object you must ask yourself many questions about the object's appearance. These should include questions as to its textures, such as these: Is it rough? What causes its rough appearance? How can I suggest this roughness? Is it smooth? Why does it look smooth? How can I paint it to look smooth? Is it shiny? Is it so shiny that it mirrors other objects? How can I make it look shiny? Must I paint the mirrored objects? How can I suggest these features, this vine-clad wall, the bark of this tree?

There are dozens of such questions and dozens of answers. Successful texture indication starts with successful observation of the textures of the objects themselves, as they appear from the spectator's point of view. Usually textural appearances result from millions of dots or lines of tone or color, or of tiny light and shade areas. Each hair in a piece of fur, for example, not only has its own innate colors and values, but also its areas of light, shade, and shadow, so the fur reveals even to our imperfect human eyesight a multitude of almost infinitesimal details.

### EXPERIMENT WITH TEXTURES

Inasmuch as no one could paint every one of these tiny effects, it must be obvious that when we represent objects—sometimes huge objects—within the narrow confines of our canvas, we can at best only indicate or suggest their textures. Textures, by the way, are not limited to individual small things. We have just hinted that a vine-clad wall has its texture; so does the foliage of a tree. A distant tree-covered mountainside has its texture, too—perhaps a very variegated one. A wheat field at some distance likewise has its texture just as definite as that of a single leaf or blade of grass near-by. We repeat that there can be no rules for handling such diverse appearances. The artist must normally experiment with the indication of a certain texture until, largely by trial and error, he gets it to look right. The next time, he knows how to do it. But no one —no book—can tell him.

Sometimes, if objects are rough, the selection of rough canvas for their depiction is a step in the right direction. Again, the kind of brush chosen makes a great difference. Often the manner in which the brush is manipulated—the way in which its strokes are made—is an important factor. Through dragging a stiff brush across a painted surface or dabbing the surface with the bristles, through working one color into another with the finger, through wiping off with a rag, through painting knife manipulation, even through such occasional experiments as scraping or sandpapering, are textural effects obtained.

The experiments illustrated by Figure 29 point the way to reader experimentation with textures. In the case of realistic renderings of still life, objects are often pictured at actual size, or nearly so. Their textures can therefore be represented quite literally.

In rendering the glass at A, for example—a type of object in which we broaden the definition of the word "texture" to include the various reflections which give the object a shiny appearance—the mere pictorial recording of the form, values and color of the glass automatically recorded both its shine and its transparency. This study, by the way, is of a painstaking, somewhat photographic type which the beginner can do to advantage at this time. As he becomes more proficient, he will learn to dash off his results with greater facility, emphasizing the larger masses and sacrificing (simplifying or omitting) lesser details. To make his glass

*Figure 29*

**TEXTURES** *One of your daily problems in painting will be to represent satisfactorily the textures of all types of subject matter.*

100

A

shine, he will eventually quite likely use quick painted strokes, for glassy surfaces can customarily be best represented in this way.

The antique powder horn at B offered a far from easy problem, for not only were normal light and shade evident, but the inherent tone of the horn was somewhat complicated, shading from very light areas to very dark areas. In other words, it was hard, when viewing the object, to differentiate between the local values and those resulting from light and shade. All values were of course painted simultaneously; the direction of the brush strokes, following the direction of growth of the horn, expressed both the values and textures.

So, to repeat, in rendering such still life objects, textures often take care of themselves if the forms are logically expressed.

It is when we turn outdoors (or to large subjects indoors) that we find that textures, instead of being so literally interpreted, must normally be indicated or suggested, unless, as was the case in painting the flower at C, the object is near at hand or small in size. (The petals of this flower, by the way, left no doubt as to logical brush direction.) In the sketch at D, representing a rotting tree stump some three or four feet high, surrounded by thousands of leaves and small branches, the subject on canvas has been reduced to but a few inches in height. Many outdoor subjects—distant mountains for instance—similarly shrink on canvas to a very small proportion of the original size. With this in mind, it is obvious that it is impossible for the artist to paint all the millions of tiny areas of light, dark or color which constitute the scene before him; he must suggest them. This is particularly true of their textures. Leaves, grass, rocks —everything which is included—must be rendered as to create the needed illusion of form, values, colors and textures. Only through first-hand experimentation can one master all this.

One word of caution as to textures. Don't make either your means or your textural results too plainly evident in the finished work. Never

should the spectator be unduly aware of the various textural manifestations exhibited by your final painting, or the means of obtaining them.

*Exercise 24: Texture indication*
Why not make a few small paintings, perhaps of simple objects which reveal outstanding textural characteristics? This will not only sharpen your awareness of such textures, but will help you learn to indicate or suggest them. Sometimes it is well to make your first such studies in a single dark color—umber (mixed with white as needed) is good. This working in monochrome permits you to forget color considerations for a moment and to concentrate instead on the one matter of texture representation. Later, when it comes to outdoor work, make similar studies in the indication of textures of large subjects as reduced to fit your canvas.

### STUDYING THE OLD MASTERS

The old masters were masters in every sense, and many a lesson can be learned from a careful examination of their work. When this is not available in the original, good photographs, even in black and white, can be of help.

### ANOTHER MEANING

We should not leave this subject without reference to another use of the word "texture." The artist, through the roughness of his canvas, through the quality and disposition of his brush strokes, through the interweaving of his colors, and perhaps through the very nature of his subject matter, often develops in his painting a quality which is called, for lack of a better term, "texture." Recognizing this quality, we say, "This painting has texture." It is one of the subtle, hard-to-define terms in Art. A painting need not be rough to have texture; it need not be smooth; it need not represent the textures of nature. See if you can recognize this quality in some paintings, despite our inability to define it more precisely in words.

*102*

# Chapter 9

OUR PURPOSE IN this chapter is to follow through, from the selection of the subject matter to the painting of the finishing touches, the realistic rendering in oil of a simple still life.

### CHOICE OF SUBJECT

Four objects were chosen: an ancient jug (unearthed from the cellar) bearing a shellac label, a paintbrush, and a broken cup containing a smaller paintbrush. These lend themselves to a pleasing composition, and for a number of reasons. First, they are related by use. Second, to some degree they are related in form (having both straight lines and curves), yet are sufficiently varied in both form and size. Speaking of size, the jug is large enough to dominate the composition; when two or three objects are of equal size they may fight for attention. Third, the objects offer contrasts in value ranging the whole way from the white of the cup to the black of the paintbrush hairs and the extreme dark brown of the glaze of the jug top. There is sufficient variety of texture to pose challenging problems in delineation yet without proving confusing. As to color, there is very little; we have seen that this is an advantage in some early problems as it forces one to concentrate on the all-important matter of values of light and dark.

*Figure 30*
STILL LIFE SET-UP  *The objects to be painted have been grouped here in a unified arrangement, and simply lighted from the left.*

COMPOSITION

With the objects selected, a small table was placed against a wall some six or eight feet from a window. The table was covered with a white cloth. Grayish-brown cardboard was chosen as a suitable vertical background, light enough to afford ample contrast with the darker values yet dark enough to throw the cup and other light tones into relief. A blind was drawn to cover the upper half of the window in an attempt to simplify the light, shade and shadow. Then the objects were moved here and there in an effort to create a unified composition. At least a dozen arrangements were tried, each being studied with the aid of a view finder.

Note that the objects as finally arranged form, roughly, a triangle, with the larger brush its horizontal base. Such a composition is restful. In direct opposition to the horizontal lines of the brush are the verticals of the jug. The small brush in the cup is an important element because it ties the cup into the group. The lights and darks are well distributed, light against dark and dark against light, so that the whole forms a pleasing pattern or design on the canvas. The shadows are another important unifying factor, as is the case with many compositions. These objects, thus composed, might have been used for either a vertical or a horizontal picture, though the latter seems more logical.

In arranging such objects, quickly drawn small sketches can often prove of great help; these are often called "thumbnails" because of their diminutive size. Make a sketch of one arrangement, then rearrange the objects and do a second sketch, and so on. By comparing the sketches,

*104*

you can decide on the best final composition. Such sketches will not only help you to visualize the compositional possibilities of your subject matter, but will clarify your intention in regard to its proper pictorial representation.

**STEP ONE: FIRST STAGE**

With the palette set with the few needed colors, a 12 x 16 inch canvas was chosen, and the subject was very lightly sketched in a charcoal outline at nearly actual size. No attempt was made to copy the proportions slavishly; on the other hand, inasmuch as they looked reasonably satisfactory in the subject, practically no deliberate alteration was done, excepting to narrow the cup slightly as it seemed glaringly white (this was perhaps a mistake, as the original shape, with more flare at the top, is more pleasing), and to extend the brush a bit further to the left to form an overall proportion more like that of the canvas area.

The charcoal lines were then dusted off with a rag until barely visible. These lines were then hastily reinforced with a bit of burnt umber diluted with turpentine, as indicated in Figure 31. With this same mixture, plus a small amount of white, the painting was then carried to the stage shown in this illustration.

*Figure 31*
**STEP ONE** *In the first stage, the subjects are sketched on the canvas and the larger masses of light and dark are roughly defined.*

At this time, large areas of the canvas were left bare, as the lighter values of the subject were such that they could be quite well indicated by the canvas alone. Enough was done, however, to give a complete general impression of the subject, with its leading light, shade and shadow areas established. (Perhaps we should remind the reader that it is considered better practice, generally speaking, to cover the entire canvas fully, and soon, using plenty of colors approximating those of the subject.)

### MODELING

Because a realistic effect was sought, as the painting was gradually developed much emphasis was placed on trying to make the objects come forward from the canvas—to give them a three-dimensional quality, their form in space. Another aim was to produce an effect of weight—to make plain that the objects were resting firmly on the table; the shadows underneath help to create this effect.

Despite the apparent casualness of this first stage study (Figure 31), don't let it fool you; there is plenty of knowledge and thinking behind it. Put all the time and thought on your own studies that you think necessary, for the more you can absorb at this early stage of the form and spirit of your subject matter, the more successful will be your final painting. Try especially to get in mind (and in your sketch) the chief areas or divisions of light, shade, and shadow. Squint at your setup with eyes nearly closed, and thus see it in simplified form, with light and dark areas defined. Often, by the way, it is a good idea to make a careful charcoal drawing of your entire subject at this time as a preliminary to further work on your canvas. Remember an advantage of charcoal is that it is rapid and permits easy changes.

### STEP TWO: INTERMEDIATE STAGE

Obviously paintings do not progress by two or three definite stages. There is gradual development; one works first here and then there, jumping back and forth so as to keep the whole thing coming and to utilize to best advantage the paint at the moment on his brush. (Unless a subject is extremely simple, don't make the mistake of completing one object—or one part of your painting—at a time.)

*Figure 32*
STEP TWO *In the second stage, all parts of the subject are advanced simultaneously. Never complete one part at a time.*

In the stage pictured as Figure 32, the darkest darks were boldly, if somewhat hastily, established. Most teachers feel that it is better to do this than to start more timidly with lighter, more tentative values, then adding darker and darker tones by degrees. Certainly the bold approach saves time—and paint. Perhaps even more important, it forces you to decide on the real essentials of your subject and to record them on your canvas while in your first minutes of creative drive. This direct procedure prepares you, also, for later outdoor work when speed is so often essential in order to record nature's ever-changing effects.

Shadows, by the way, not only play a large part in your composition of light and dark; when it comes to color, they supply great depth and interest. If your light comes from the north, your shadows will doubtless tend to be warm, and vice versa.

*107*

Often, a painting is at its best in some respects at about this stage. It has dash, vitality, a spontaneous quality which is often lost as one begins to "slick up." Thus the painting in Figure 32 is better in some ways than the rather overworked final result shown as Figure 33.

### STEP THREE: FINAL STAGE

Now begin the careful refinement and readjustment; the lightening of one tone and the darkening of another; the sharpening of certain edges and the softening or blurring of others; the addition of strokes designed to express the textures of different surfaces.

This means that you should frequently stand your subject and painting side by side, examining, comparing, weighing. At about this point, the experienced painter often purposely begins to make things somewhat different from what they are in the subject. In our example as shown in the photograph, Figure 30, for instance, the shadows were, to a degree, double shadows caused by light from two sources (see double shadow of smaller brush handle). These were simplified in the painting. The cup shadow on the horizontal supporting plane was extended to the background, and the entire vertical background tone was lightened towards the top. The handle of the brush in the cup was lightened, too, not only

*Figure 33*

**STEP THREE** *By gradual degrees, the entire painting is brought toward completion, until at last the finishing touches are added.*

to bring it forward, but so as to use it as a more conspicuous link to tie the cup and jug together. No effort was made to duplicate all of the minor details on the jug. Even in such carefully finished work, one goes after big impressions, not trifling detail.

### LOST EDGES

Note that the jug at the right so merges with the shadow that it is hard to follow its vertical edge for its entire length. Don't be afraid to "lose" edges in this way. Too many beginners try to make every part of their subject stand out, whether or not it does so in nature. It is only by "sacrificing" some areas in shadow that the parts in light can be brought forward to create a three-dimensional impression.

*Exercise 25: Still life*
We urge you at this time to undertake a number of still life subjects, varying them greatly in nature.

### A WORD OF WARNING

As a painting approaches its final stage the beginner may try to lighten tones which are overdark by painting white directly into them on the canvas. Seldom is this practical. It is far better to mix on your palette fresh paint of the proper hue. An excess of white, particularly when brushed on in this manner, can produce an artificial, unpleasant, chalky effect. Above all, keep white out of your shadows. Save it for your highlights; even these are often better when slightly tinted. With this in mind, study original oil paintings in the galleries and museums. Hold a piece of white paper against them. You may be surprised to learn how seldom any absolute white will be found. This is also true of black.

# Chapter 10

INDOOR
PREPARATION
FOR
OUTDOOR WORK

ONCE YOU HAVE gained familiarity with the handling of all of your painting materials, and have acquired something of a grasp of the representation
of forms, colors, values, and textures, you are ready to attempt to paint
any kind of subject matter, whether indoors or out. Many of you will
now want to step into the open to undertake your first subjects there,
whether they be landscapes, marines, street scenes, buildings old or new,
or such living things as animals and people. Chapter 11 deals with these
ventures out-of-doors.

It sometimes happens, however, that one is ready to embark on these
initial outdoor painting efforts in the winter, just when nature is doing
her best to discourage such activities. What is he to do? He may have
the opportunity and means to seek a sunny clime. But, if not, must he kill
a month or two waiting for spring? Or are there further types of
preparatory work which he can attempt?

*Exercise 26: Indoor preparation*
It should be obvious that the painter can improve his time in any of a
dozen ways, but let's look at a few possibilities. First, why not try some
winter landscapes? They have much to commend them, and often they
can be done in comfort and security from a window of one's own home;

this is especially true in these days of "picture" windows. Certain types of subject matter can be studied to unusual advantage in winter. Deciduous trees, for example, being bare of leaves, offer the opportunity to become familiar with their skeletons of trunks and branches. Colors in winter are varied, too, and far more in evidence than is sometimes realized. Effects of snow and ice present many a challenge; it will be found that snow is by no means a thing of absolute white. And shadow shapes can be studied to advantage in winter, as they are especially evident where they fall on snow-covered surfaces.

### PAINTING IN AN AUTOMOBILE

If one would go further afield, sitting in a heated automobile gives opportunities such as never before existed to reach many a fine subject and to paint it from a haven which can usually be kept comparatively comfortable even on days of extremely low temperature.

### PAINTING FROM PHOTOGRAPHS

But there are plenty of other things which can be done, even after dark. Not long ago, I had a winter evening class of students, many of whom were anxious to prepare themselves for summer landscape work. For a number of sessions we concentrated on studying and painting skies and clouds, obtaining suggestions from projected films or slides, photographs and colored prints, many of the latter reproducing the work of outstanding painters. Using similar source material, we then looked into the subject of trees, shrubs, flowers, grass and the like. Again, we worked at rocks, ledges, cliffs, and mountains. Such things as waves, waterfalls, rivers, lakes, wet streets and beaches proved intriguing; we even experimented with effects of fog and rain. Different reflections as seen mirrored on wet surfaces were studied in this connection. Several profitable sessions were given to analyzing and representing buildings and such of their details as glass, stonework and brickwork.

Perhaps our greatest gain in this class came from the photographs in natural color which we projected onto the screen; from these we learned an amazing amount about nature's astonishing variety of appearances. We observed how all sorts of subject matter looked, whether in the foreground, middle distance, or distance. More than once we even painted directly from such projected material, which, despite a certain amount of distortion of both form and color, gave us a remarkable sense of working out-of-doors. In some instances, a dozen or more students painted from the same projected image. Now and then the projector was turned off for a few minutes and the paintings-in-progress were placed side by side for comparison, comments being volunteered by all. This proved most helpful; each student learned from all the others.

Also, it cannot be denied that one can occasionally benefit a great deal through working (in color) from a good black-and-white photograph, or, for that matter, from copying intelligently an original painting or good color reproduction. In such work, don't paint on too small a scale, and don't copy slavishly. Merely go after the main impression in the shortest possible time, imagining that you are working from the actual outdoor subject matter. And never imitate the mannerisms of any one painter; as insurance against this, don't as a rule copy more than a single example of any one painter's work. For that matter, do but a few copies altogether or you may form a very dangerous habit.

### USING REPRODUCTIONS

Supplementing such classroom activities, the inclement winter months give the much needed time for visits to galleries and museums. (On such visits, by the way, don't fail to observe how important is the subject of picture framing. A good frame can do much to enhance your picture; on the other hand, the wrong frame may detract from it.) Lacking opportunities for such visits, study good reproductions of the work of our master painters past and present. Books of collections such as *Art Treasures of The Louvre* by René Huyghe (Harry N. Abrams Inc.) and *A Treasury of Art Masterpieces* by Thomas Craven (Simon & Schuster) can inspire you, on the one hand, while opening your eyes to many a matter you need to know about. Volumes on appreciation are also eye-openers in a somewhat different way. The American classic in this field still seems to be *The Art Spirit* by Robert Henri (Lippincott). Don't fail to read it. You may also want something on modern art. And, as a painter, you'll need to know your art history, no matter how modern your viewpoint. In this connection, *Art through the Ages* by Helen Gardner (Harcourt, Brace & World) can be recommended as another standard work. So borrow, beg or buy some good art books; you'll never regret it.

Above, we spoke of framing. If you wish a good book on this subject, we suggest *How to Make Your Own Picture Frames* by Hal Rogers and Ed Reinhardt (Watson-Guptill).

Speaking of books, don't forget the technical books—the how-to-do-it type. It has been my experience that no two such books give precisely the same instruction or present the same point of view. Therefore, acquire all of the painting books you can afford, remembering that if you get a few truly worthwhile ideas from each, they will be well worth the purchase price, for you will utilize such facts throughout your painting career.

As a closing thought, remember that there's no such thing as being able to draw or paint too well. Why not join a life, figure, or portrait class, or do some still-life or flower painting while you are waiting for spring to open up the great out-of-doors? Or perhaps you prefer to improve your knowledge of such subjects as composition, anatomy and perspective. You may be sure that every hour that you can devote to such effort will pay you generously when at last you step into the open, paintbox in hand.

# Chapter 11

## YOUR FIRST OUTDOOR PICTURE

WITH SUCH A background as you should have acquired by now, you are well prepared to venture into the open. But before you pick up your brushes to paint your first outdoor picture, it would be well for you to have in mind a clear purpose and plan. Different people by no means have the same conception as to what they want to do with their paints. A majority of beginners, and some professionals, apparently desire to produce very realistic pictures of actual persons, places, or things—pictures almost photographically exact. The closer they can come to nature's appearances, the happier they will be. *Such artists are pictorial reporters, recorders of visual appearances.*

There are other painters—especially among the more advanced— who approach picturemaking in a more creative manner; they like to select various details or effects from nature, altering and combining them to suit their individual fancy, weaving them, as it were, into a unified pictorial whole, with each element properly related to every other element. They may considerably exaggerate or distort certain elements in order to give them emphasis. While their pictures may be convincingly naturalistic in general effect, they will not as a rule be true representations of subjects which actually exist. *Such artists are translators, interpreters, to some extent creators.*

*Hobart Nichols:* SUNSHINE AND CABBAGES    *The rows of cabbages indicate how the rules of perspective can be applied in the rolling form of the land. The blue distant hills are examples of atmospheric perspective. Remember, distant objects are paler than objects near-by. Courtesy, Grand Central Art Galleries.*

Still other artists merely draw their inspiration—or a part of it—from nature, or borrow motives which they interpret with even greater freedom. Rather than being painters some of these are, in a broad sense, designers. They view each canvas less as an area to fill with a picture than as a space to turn into a design or pattern. They don't mind what others frequently consider inconsistencies, distortions, faults of perspective, errors of proportion and the like; often they purposely create them. They may merely "spot" their canvas effectively with conventionalized shapes or areas of color which bear little if any resemblance to those of nature. Abstractionists and nonobjective painters often fall within this category.

In the following chapters, I am assuming that most of you are in the first or second of the above classes. You prefer a somewhat realistic approach, and hope that your finished paintings will give reasonably close impressions of nature. Many of them will represent actual persons, places or things, with or without some modifications of your own.

### CHOICE OF SUBJECT

If you are to get real fun from your work and at the same time accomplish results appealing to others, you will seek interesting subjects to paint. I have repeatedly mentioned that many beginners like to paint out-of-doors, doing landscapes, marines, street scenes, picturesque old buildings, etc. Some prefer people or animals. Others may choose things indoors, such as room interiors, still life, fruit, flowers. Practically all of us have a preference for subject matter which we consider pleasing in appearance, with shapes and textures which are attractive, and with colors which delight the eye. We like well-arranged groupings of flowers, satisfying dispositions of trees and mountains, people with character. On the other hand there are those who deliberately choose subject matter which is broken down or dilapidated, depressing and unpleasant in appearance: dead trees, tumble-down tenements with woebegone occupants, lonely bits of countryside, hungry dogs, dirt and filth. They represent what has so aptly been termed the "ash-can" school of art. The person who likes to paint an attractive country lane would perhaps find it uninspiring to represent battered garbage cans. So each to his own choice; all types of subjects have great possibilities to those who have the vision to see them.

People vary greatly in their ability to discover subjects to their liking. Some students—and an occasional professional—spend hours wandering around the countryside seeking in vain a satisfactory bit of nature to portray. Nature apparently confuses them with the grandness of her displays and the lavishness of her offerings. Others, more discerning, set up their easels almost anywhere, finding subjects galore.

Don't feel that you must locate the "perfect" subject—a ready-made picture waiting to be "copied." Seldom will you be so fortunate. Almost anything will serve at first if it shows definite contrast of form and color and holds some degree of interest or appeal. The beginner usually finds it easier to do things at a little distance, as near-by subjects reveal so much detail that they prove confusing; also their perspective is more acute and more difficult to interpret. (In order to see an entire subject near-by, it often becomes necessary to shift the eye constantly, looking up, down, right, and left from minute to minute. With each such move, the subject changes in proportion—it really forms a new picture. When, on the other hand, a subject is at a great distance, one can see it as a whole without shifting the eye, which makes it much easier to comprehend and record.)

### DON'T ATTEMPT TOO MUCH

Almost invariably the beginner undertakes something far more difficult or complex than he is capable of doing well. He would like to get into every picture too many of the things which he sees about him. He may therefore spend hours in trying to draw the complicated proportions properly and in getting under way with the first work with his brush, only to find that time has run out. Or he may become so lost in a maze of details, and so puzzled by problems of color, composition, etc., that he grows very discouraged.

Don't make this mistake. One of your aims is relaxation and pleasure, which you will more likely get if you select something small or simple. Remember this advice of a very wise teacher: "Don't try to paint all outdoors in one picture. Leave something for *next* time."

If you *do* undertake a rather large or complex subject, don't hope to create more than a general impression of it. If your proportions aren't just right, that's not too serious. If some of the colors don't quite suit, you needn't judge them harshly. If you can't seem to represent every detail of nature convincingly, you mustn't be too disturbed.

I am by no means suggesting that you should approach your task casually, for you will want to give it your best effort. What I am trying to make clear is that you are, after all, but a novice; you can't expect to possess too much proficiency. You wouldn't hope to play the piano at your first attempt, and painting calls for a somewhat similar degree of skill. Gradually you will learn to profit from your mistakes.

Is it any satisfaction to know that even the experienced painter often feels dissatisfied with his initial interpretation of a subject out-of-doors? He may repaint passages again and again before he captures the effect he seeks. He may even fail to capture it at all!

Some painters never finish any work directly from nature; many of their landscapes—even those which give the appearance of having been dashed off spontaneously on the site—are actually painstakingly built up in the studio from quick sketches, studies, and notes previously made in the field. In each of these field sketches and studies, the artist tries to record certain main characteristics of some subject which appeals to him—its form, its play of light and shade, its color, or its mood—knowing that he may later utilize this data in a studio painting. Often in his final painting he combines portions of a number of these outdoor sketches and studies, perhaps altering or distorting some of them in order to give emphasis to his main idea. In other words, he exercises his prerogative to amalgamate into a unified whole many elements or characteristics of his preliminary work, relying on his memory as a supplementary source of inspiration and information. This is where the creative phase which we have mentioned comes in—the composing of a painting which may not represent any one actual place or moment of time but which is, instead, largely the invention of the artist.

### NATURE IS FICKLE

A main reason why it is seldom practical to try to make a finished painting of any great magnitude out-of-doors—even if one would like to—is that it is humanly impossible to work fast enough to finish a subject before its appearance changes. Nature's effects are transient. The sun may fall on one side of a building when the artist starts to lay out his work, yet within an hour it may shine on another side, for its movement is surprisingly rapid. Clouds obscure the sun only to pass away again; cloud shadows chase one another across the landscape, affecting light, shade and color. At times the wind blows the trees or ripples the water; again,

118

all is calm. The mists which one sees in early morning, veiling the subject matter (particularly in the distance), gradually burn away. Smoke may modify the picture from moment to moment.

If you wish to gain a full realization of how frequent and rapid such changes are, make a series of snapshots of any given subject at periods an hour or so apart throughout an entire day, all of them from precisely the same position and using the same focus and exposure. Not only will these photographs vary greatly in effect, but one or two of them are practically certain to be esthetically more successful than the rest.

### VIEW FINDER

Just as the photographer utilizes the view finder on his camera in choosing a suitable subject, and in determining the best station point from which to photograph it, so the painter relies on a simple little handmade gadget devised for the same purpose and called by the same name. Such a gadget consists of a bit of stiff white cardboard, postcard size or so, with a rectangular aperture through which he can study various potential subjects, peeking at each (with one eye closed) from several positions in order to discover the most favorable point of view. The opening can measure about an inch by an inch and a quarter—larger if one wishes—to approximate the proportions of his canvas. Under normal conditions the cardboard is held vertically a few inches from the eye. The opening may of course be either upright or horizontal, according to whether one desires to paint a vertical or a horizontal picture.

### TIME OF DAY

What we just said about a series of photographs stresses the fact that there is an ideal time of day for painting almost any subject in nature. A subject which seems unattractive at noon may look very pleasing in early morning or late afternoon, much depending on the nature and direction of the light. Indoors, it is often possible for the artist to arrange his own lighting but out-of-doors he must wait for nature to give him the best arrangement. Naturally, the more pleasing the lighting on a subject the more satisfactory the painting will be. Sometimes an artist returns to a site at the same hour for several days in order to work under approximately the same lighting conditions. Even then he will seldom if ever find effects precisely duplicated.

It is not enough for you to discover a suitable subject, favorably lighted, and the best position from which to view it. It is also essential to locate a practical spot in which to set up your canvas. The more comfortable you are, the more likely you will be to produce a good picture. Some painters almost invariably select a shady place, or at least make certain that there is no glare of light and that their canvas is not in direct sunshine, as it is difficult to judge what one is doing unless his working surface is shaded. An artist's umbrella is sometimes useful. Many painters like to sit, which means that they must either bring a suitable stool or hunt up some seat which will provide reasonable comfort. (An old newspaper or magazine affords fair protection against dampness.) As you will probably remain in the same position for at least a couple of hours, you will want to consider such factors as probable change in the direction of the sun, wind, etc. If it is very windy and you are using an easel, make sure that it is properly anchored.

**ANALYSIS OF SUBJECT**

As in the case of your previous still life painting, analyze every part of your subject before undertaking any work on your canvas. Is it short or tall? Rounded or angular? Rough or smooth in texture? Strong or weak in contrasts of light and dark? Bright or dull in color? Acute or restful in perspective? In short, what are its main appearance characteristics? Remember that most subjects appeal to us because of certain desirable characteristics which can be stressed in a painting, less vital ones being subordinated or omitted.

**PRELIMINARY SKETCHES**

Let me once more point out that in order to plan your work—to learn ahead of time how the selected material can be utilized pictorially to best advantage—it is often well to make preliminary sketches in charcoal or pencil. A sketchbook is excellent for this purpose. First rough out what seems to be a logical boundary of the limits of your intended picture, locating this on your paper as a rectangle which has about the proportions of a typical canvas. For example, if you plan to paint a 16 x 20 inch canvas, your preliminary sketch might be 4 x 5 inches or 8 x 10 inches.

*Figure 34*
THUMBNAIL SKETCH  *A pencil was used for this sketch, which was no more than five inches wide.*

Then, within this area sketch the leading proportions of your subject and, when they are reasonably correct, rough in the light and shade. In such a preliminary sketch you have a simplified guide for your work on canvas. The accompanying thumbnail sketch (Figure 34) is typical of what I have in mind. It measured five inches in width.

### CROPPING

Just as one can often crop photographs to advantage by hiding or cutting away undesirable areas, so one can frequently crop the subjects as first sketched. Test this. After you have made your little sketch, experiment by laying strips of paper over the edges (or by looking at your work through your finder). Perhaps you have sketched an entire barn. You may note that by letting a portion of this barn run out of the picture the effect is improved.

### SKETCHING ON CANVAS

You are now ready to lay out your subject on canvas. Obviously, the more you know of the principles and practices of freehand drawing, the more easily you can record the material before you. But remember, you aren't to worry too much as to the perfection of your layout. As we earlier mentioned, some beginners fritter away a whole morning either trying to find a subject or attempting to decide how to utilize it. Others spend several hours blocking out their subject, and so have no time left to paint. *The main thing is to pitch in boldly—to get paint on your canvas without much delay.*

121

The sketching on the canvas may be done with pencil, charcoal, or brush. If the latter is chosen, the paint may be of any color, as we saw in discussing still life subjects. Usually something neutral—brown or gray in general effect—is advisable. Some artists like gray-blue. A brush with a point fine enough to draw a narrow line should be held freely, with the hand well back from the metal ferrule. The canvas should be upright on the easel so as to be viewed approximately at right angles.

If you sketch on your canvas with graphite pencil, keep your lines extremely light and don't use too soft a grade of graphite, for the softer it is, the more it will tend to dissolve when the turpentine or other medium strikes it. It may then streak and spread annoyingly. When charcoal is used, once the general proportions have been satisfactorily determined, dust off any excess with a cloth or chamois. Some artists spray their charcoal or pencil work with fixative. Others feel that it is better not to use fixative, unless very sparingly, fearing that it may not form a durable base for the oil painting to follow.

### LINEAR VS. TONAL CONSTRUCTION

For most of us it is natural in such construction work, whether in the sketchbook or on the canvas, to draw in outline, bounding the major areas with lines. Nature, however, uses no outline; we distinguish one object from another only because it is lighter or darker in tone or of a different color. Some painters therefore prefer to draw or paint their construction layout directly in tone. If they choose paint, they customarily use a wider brush than for linear work and actually fill in (with greatly diluted neutral or lightly tinted paint) the larger areas, thus getting some tone all over the canvas as soon as possible, each area approximating in shape its counterpart in nature.

It doesn't matter too much whether you use a linear or tonal approach; you should work in the most natural way—you may wish to combine the two. The main thing, I repeat, is to get on your canvas an impression (subject, of course, to gradual later correction) of your subject. This gives you something to analyze before going on.

### SPEED

In all this preliminary study, as in the painting to follow, work rapidly, keeping in mind that nature's effects are ephemeral.

**PROCEDURE**

With your subject constructed, you are now ready to shoot ahead. Perhaps the best way to guide you in this is to refer you to the step-by-step demonstration offered in the next chapter. Read this now, if you wish. We shall then digress a bit (Chapter 13) but shall return in Chapter 14 to our present line of thought.

# Chapter 12

## A LANDSCAPE
## STEP-BY-STEP

AT THIS POINT it seems logical to follow the painting of a simple landscape subject from start to finish, just as we did in the case of the still life in Chapter 9.

### CHOOSING THE SUBJECT

The subject chosen (Figure 35)—an old barn on an abandoned farm in upstate New York—is a good one, and for a number of reasons. First, it is relatively simple in its elements; it explains itself—there is nothing to wonder about. The interest naturally focuses on the dilapidated barn, darkly silhouetted against a light sky. The opened doors create a focal area of light surrounded by dark. This sagging structure is so distorted in form through settling that it matters little just how the proportions are drawn—another advantage to the beginner who can't draw well! The arrangement of the surroundings is pleasing, with the shapes and values nicely distributed. As to color, the barn was a natural weathered gray, and the sky a clear blue, almost cerulean. The trees and grass showed the commonplace and somewhat monotonous greens of early summer, so they suggested modification in the direction of greater variety.

*Figure 35*

LANDSCAPE *By choosing this angle, the artist was able to paint in the shade.*

**STATION POINT**

The artist, having studied the subject from various distances and at different angles, chose the view shown in the photograph, Figure 35, as the best. He was able to place his easel in shade.

**STEP ONE: FIRST STAGE**

The subject was sketched on a 12 x 16 inch canvas panel directly with the brush, the paint being burnt umber diluted with turpentine. In but a few minutes the whole thing was roughed out as it appears in Figure 36, just enough tone being applied to establish the leading areas. As this

*Figure 36*

STEP ONE *In this first stage, the subject has been blocked out very freely and quickly. Much of the canvas has been left blank. Speed is almost an essential in landscape work because effects change often.*

value arrangement, with its light foreground, has much to commend it, it was decided to use it (with modifications) for the final painting. It has one definite factor in its favor: it prevents the square of light seen through the open doorways from becoming as overconspicuous as it does in the photograph and in our study, Figure 39.

### STEP TWO: INTERMEDIATE STAGE

In the second stage (Figure 37), the sky was first roughed in. This is often a good move, and for several reasons. First, the sky is a luminous thing with a value which often gives the key to one's entire subject. Once you paint your sky, you can relate everything else to it. Second, it is much easier, as a rule, to paint such details as tree branches and foliage masses against the completed sky than it is to fit patches of sky between or around them. As a minor third point, if you wait to paint your sky last, you may—unless you hold your brush well extended—get your hand or sleeve in the rest of the work below. In our present subject it was important to keep the sky very light and luminous in order to silhouette the barn against it successfully.

With the sky values determined, some color was added throughout the canvas. The barn was nearly completed next, with further toning of the trees and grass. The tree mass at the left was painted in gray green, considerably duller than nature showed, and the foliage immediately below the open doorway was made quite colorful with reds and reddish

*Figure 37*

**STEP TWO**  *The second step was to add more color throughout. As the greens in the subject were monotonous, liberties were taken in the painting. Incidentally, the painting was done in one hour.*

browns not present in the subject. Details like the daisies were saved until the final stage. Such things can easily demand too much attention.

Sometimes, of course, a subject like these daisies can be featured. (I might add, parenthetically, that this area near Argyle, New York, while not well-known to painters, has much to recommend it. Not only do the Argyle Hills offer wide views of the upper Hudson Valley, with the Adirondacks stacking up in the northwest and the Green Mountains in the east, but they provide more intimate views of steep hills and narrow valleys.)

### STEP THREE: FINAL STAGE

As this painting in its preliminary stages gave a fresh, spontaneous impression, it was decided not to carry it too far in the final. In this final stage, therefore (Figure 38), only enough was done to round out a reasonably well-balanced composition. The sky was slicked up a bit, the values of the barn were adjusted, the distant trees were given a more pleasing contour, and such details as the foreground grass and daisies were added. Adjustments and refinements are still needed, though.

### STUDIO STUDY

The somewhat recomposed study reproduced as Figure 39 was later done in the studio (it measured only 6 inches in height) with the thoughts of

*Figure 38*
**STEP THREE** *In this third stage, inasmuch as the early work seemed to catch the mood of the subject quite successfully, only enough adjustments were made to improve the composition in minor details.*

*Figure 39*

STUDIO STUDY  *This painting was later done in the studio as an experiment in recomposition.*

basing a painting upon it. While the black-and-white reproduction fails to do justice to the rich tones of the original, this study has a glaring fault. Not only is the light area through the doorway disturbingly prominent (it could, of course, be toned down along with nearby sky areas), but this area unfortunately falls in the precise center of the picture (as it does in Figure 38, for that matter). When such a fault is recognized, however, it is not hard to correct it, and a successful painting could be based on this study.

Note, incidentally, that the trees in the distant right have again been made quite different in form and value from those in the original subject. This is doubtless an improvement. They were changed in color, also, all of which increased the sense of distance.

### CROPPING

When such a disturbing factor as the light spot just mentioned reveals itself, the artist often resorts to the expedient of cropping his painting.

*128*

*Figure 40*
STUDIO STUDY CROPPED
*The studio study in
Figure 39 was cropped at
bottom and left, largely
because the door openings
formed a conspicuous spot
precisely in the center
of the painting.*

In the present case, part of the somewhat empty foreground of Figure 39 could be cut away, or the subject could be trimmed at the left, or both. Here, however, as in most cases of cropping, some relatively minor adjustments of forms, values or colors could advantageously be done if the subject were cropped as indicated.

We have already seen that this combining into a single picture of elements from several sketches or studies—or from memory—is common. In this present case it was unnecessary, as the subject was already well-composed. A lot of subjects, however, can be greatly improved by such means.

WHEN YOU ENLARGE

Many a sketch which seems very satisfactory at small scale proves disappointing when enlarged into a studio painting. This is because certain areas, when expanded, look empty and uninteresting. The artist often has to use considerable ingenuity to increase the interest in such areas without cluttering the composition with too many competing elements or trivial details. But if you enlarge a subject and it looks empty don't be too hasty in adding material. You may soon decide that the subject, as enlarged, isn't empty or dreary after all.

*Exercise 27: Complete paintings*
Continuing your work as outlined in Chapter 11, bring it to conclusion as described in this chapter. Try a variety of subjects more or less in this manner.

*129*

# Chapter 13

## THE ARTIST
## A MAGICIAN

BEFORE GOING FURTHER WITH OUR "how" discussions, let's pause long enough to say a bit more about the thinking behind the doing.

We have seen that when beginners paint out-of-doors their prime purpose—aside from the fun of the thing—is usually to get to know nature more intimately, while learning to record their selected subject with reasonable fidelity. We purposely use this word "reasonable," for even if the painter so desired he could not make an absolutely truthful portrayal of any natural subject, regardless of his talent of years of experience. Even when using color photography, man can obtain only an approximation of natural appearances, and seldom can the painter—at least in a normal length of time—make as faithful a recording of the basic appearances of nature as can the camera.

If you can't truly record nature, what are you to do? As a rule, you are to create impressions or illusions of your subject matter. Such illusions can actually be far more convincing and pleasing than more literal recordings. In a sense *you can think of yourself as a magician, creating on your blank, flat canvas with your paints and brushes illusions of persons, places, or things.*

### SIZE ILLUSION

First, there is the illusion of size. Obviously, many subjects in nature are so large that it is impossible to record them at anything approaching their original dimensions. A tree, for instance, is so huge that you cannot represent all you see—every leaf and branch. You must learn the trick of indicating or suggesting the tree (with its fullness of form and its myriad details) in extremely limited space. And so it is with mountains, buildings, any large objects. In other words, you must become an expert "shrinker" of nature.

### DEPTH ILLUSION

Again, you must learn to create on the flat canvas before you an illusion of the depth and distance—the three-dimensional quality—of your subject. It is quite a trick to make the distance appear distant, to make things close at hand appear close at hand, to record each object in the right size and shape in relation to every other object so that it seems to be the proper distance from the spectator—often far beyond the plane surfaces of your canvas. Several factors enter into this bit of legerdemain.

### THE ART OF DETACHMENT

As a part of this same magic of creating illusions of distance, you must learn the art of detachment—how to picture objects so that they look separated one from another, as in nature. (By way of example, in your painting, a tree behind a building must appear actually to drop behind it, not to rest on the edge of the roof.)

### THE ILLUSION OF LIGHT

Another important part of your job as magician is to learn to give the illusion or impression of sunlight and shadow. We know that light itself is amazingly bright; we cannot look at the sun for more than an instant. Without dark glasses it is by no means easy to gaze for any length of time at a brilliantly sunlit sand beach, stucco wall, or bank of snow. One's canvas, on the contrary, is seldom viewed in sunshine, but in shade. Consequently you, the magician, must learn to create on this shaded surface the illusion of sunshine—to make some areas appear bathed in brilliant light.

### CREATING MOTION AND LIFE

Then there is the magic of suggesting motion. In nature we see a man walking through a field, or a dog running along the road. We observe the grass and the trees blowing in the wind, waving this way and that. The clouds come and go across the sky, never still for a moment. Birds fly about. It is no simple thing to learn to create on one's static canvas surface this sense of mobility—of never-ceasing movement.

In the case of living subjects, the artist must not only suggest motion but he must also try to make his subjects look alive, for, with living subjects, an appearance of animation is the essence of good painting.

### CREATING SOUND

Some paintings of active subjects—busy city streets, carnivals, or waterfronts—are successful in giving an impression of both motion and sound. Through association, the spectator, looking at such pictures, hears the shouts of the people, the music of the carousel, the tooting of whistles. Similarly, a skillful painter of flowers or gardens can sometimes bring to the spectator a sensation of fragrance.

### CREATING MOOD

This last thought brings us to one of the most difficult pieces of legerdemain of all (it really consists of many other tricks in combination)—the skill which some artists possess to an unusual degree not merely to record the physical appearance of the matter before them, but to suggest its mood. Some paintings which are reasonably accurate records of the outstanding facts of nature don't hold our interest because they have failed to catch the mood of the original subject matter. Other paintings may be faulty in certain aspects of pictorial representation, yet very successful in portraying the mood of the time and place depicted.

### IT'S NO EASY TASK

So when you go out to paint, your job is customarily not so much one of recording, camera-like, every physical aspect of your chosen subject, as it is to interpret the subject on your canvas in such a way that the spectator will be stirred emotionally more or less at your will. It is the magic with which you infuse your subject—the modifications which you invent —which makes you an artist, not a human camera. Remember that if you want to come close to an exact reproduction of nature, a camera can often do it better—and much easier—than oils.

*132*

AT THE END of Chapter 11 we left you outdoors, having completed all of your preliminaries for your first painting in the open. In Chapter 12 we demonstrated the general procedure in developing such a painting step-by-step from start to finish. We believe that this demonstration should be enough to guide you to a reasonably satisfactory conclusion of your first few paintings. As time goes on, however, you will find yourself faced with various problems not yet dealt with. It is therefore our present purpose to consider some of these, and to offer other pertinent suggestions, a part of them in amplification or review of matters earlier discussed.

### MORE ABOUT SIMPLIFICATION

We have previously indicated that almost all paintings by beginners exhibit one common fault—either the subject chosen was too complex in itself, too difficult at the start, or it was treated in too complicated a manner, so that the final work, instead of consisting of the desirable comparatively simple arrangement of relatively few values of light and dark, is needlessly broken into a confusing pattern of many small lights and darks. Sometimes the fault is with hues, rather than values: there are too many limited areas of color scattered almost hit-or-miss all over the canvas.

How is the reader to overcome or avoid such faults? How can he learn to discriminate between the essential and the incidental? Following are various suggestions. They are intended to teach him ways of reducing each subject to its lowest terms; to discover and portray the *basic elements* which give it its appeal.

### "PATTERN" SUBJECTS

Shun for the time being subjects which in themselves consist of such a variety of tones and colors—so much detail—that they are bewildering. Seek, instead, subjects which are easy to comprehend. Some of these are referred to as "pattern" subjects because they are made up of well-defined areas of tone and color. Most buildings and street scenes, for example, fall within this class, being somewhat poster-like in effect.

### POSTER TREATMENT

Speaking of posters, why not take a lesson from the poster artist, who often renders an entire landscape in but three or four tones, generally flat? He may even work in black and white alone. At the start, you can learn a lot by trying to see how well you can express a subject using only pure black and white. You need not turn to your oils for this; black ink brushed onto white paper will do. Figure 41—drawn at this exact size—shows the sort of thing we have in mind. Even so simple a result can have considerable merit; among other virtues, it proves that a great deal can

*Figure 41*
TWO VALUES  *To learn to simplify, make brush drawings like this in ink, with white for all light tones and black for all darks. Thus your subject is reduced to lowest terms.*

*Figure 42*
THREE VALUES *This little sketch was done on brownish-gray board with black ink and slightly diluted white watercolor. Learn to simplify by making such sketches.*

be expressed by the simplest of means. In Figure 42 our approach brings us a step closer to typical painting, for it was done on brownish-gray paper for the middle tones, with black ink for the darks, and a single value of slightly diluted white watercolor washed in place for the lights. Such a sketch can be a very small size. This one measured but 4¾ inches wide.

*Exercise 28: Poster studies in three values*
Try a small sketch or two in this general manner, with white for all light tones, black for all dark tones, and your middle values in a single tone of flat gray, or, at the most, in two.

*Exercise 29: Monochromatic work in oil*
Another way to learn simplicity—and this method is especially good if you are weak in your treatment of values—is to paint a few pictures with but a single oil color, darkened with black (if necessary) and lightened with white. Such a monochromatic approach will teach you to use your tools and to create your various tones and textures without the constant question of what color to choose. As to the single color, brown or brownish-gray is good, or a dull blue. Just as a black-and-white photograph can ade-

*135*

quately represent many a subject, so can such a monochromatic painting. The two are, in fact, quite similar.

*Exercise 30: Monochromatic "lay-in"*
Some painters, by the way—and this was even more true in the past—"lay in" their canvas monochromatically for every painting, attaining quite a finished effect in this manner, later repainting each area in an appropriate hue. Try this plan sometime; your work will be the better for it. (From a technical standpoint, however, this adding of color over a full range of values in monochrome might be questioned, as the monochrome, especially where extremely dark, might tend gradually to bleed through.)

*Exercise 31: Work in two colors*
Another excellent approach for those a bit timid in the use of color, on the one hand, or inclined to employ it too lavishly (but not too wisely), on the other, is to limit your palette for a while to two colors—a warm hue such as burnt sienna and a cool hue like ultramarine blue. (You may also need black and white in order to obtain a full range of values.) You will then paint all warm colors in your subject—yellows, oranges, reds, yellow-greens, etc.—with the burnt sienna and all cool colors—blues, blue-greens and blue-violets—with the ultramarine. I am not saying that you will find these fully adequate, yet you will be surprised at the richness of effect thus obtainable. Remember that the poster artist often paints a billboard satisfactorily in two or three colors. True, you aren't a billboard artist, but you have a message to get across just the same, so borrow the lesson of simplicity and directness from him. Don't, however, use flat colors for these particular exercises as he often does. Mix and modify them as freely as in any other oil work.

*Exercise 32: Three-color palette*
If you chance to be one of those who find a dozen or so paints of different hue on your palette confusing, you may like to limit yourself, for a while, to the three paint primaries, red, yellow, and blue. We have already seen that if each of these is bright and strong, reasonably close approximations of any colors found in nature can be obtained through admixture. You will learn a lot from this exercise. With three colors well understood, others can gradually be added.

I do not urge you to confine yourself to such limited palettes as any of the above; I merely suggest them to those who may be a bit bewildered by nature's chromatic profusion or by the number of colors in his own box.

### YOUR SUBJECT WILL TELL YOU

When eventually you turn to painting in full color, your palette for any given painting will obviously depend in large measure on the subject itself. For a garden or sunset scene, you may need a "full" palette of brilliant hues; a simple landscape can be done with half the number, but with more generous quantities of each. Don't be stingy!

Never, to repeat, be afraid to use dark tones. Nature seldom shows us a true black, to be sure (remember that anything which is black is veiled by atmosphere), but if your lighter colors are to count to full advantage they must be contrasted with darks. In other words, the darks are what bring emphasis to the lights. But use black, or any extremely dark tone, with discrimination.

### STAND BACK!

May I again point out that much of the beginner's trouble often comes from the fact that he stands too close to his subject. The farther away he stands, the more simple it will appear and the easier it will be to do.

### REDUCING GLASS

And get the habit of squinting at your subject frequently through partially closed lids in order to see it in simple terms. Or, study it through what is known as a "reducing glass." (Your dealer can supply it.) This has the virtue of so shrinking the subject that only its essentials are visible. Your painting can also be studied profitably from time to time through such a glass, though you may find the effect rather flattering as the poorer passages may appear less evident and disturbing than when viewed normally.

At one time there was a glass on the market which not only reduced a subject in size but, as I recall it, also blurred it somewhat, just enough to bring emphasis to essentials. As a substitute, one can rely to some extent on the ground glass of a camera.

*137*

Simplicity or complication can also result largely from good or poor use of brushes. We have already had a lot to say about brushes and the kinds and directions of brush strokes. Here are a few more thoughts:

First, we repeat our recommendation that you have several brushes (and painting knives) always at hand, choosing for each area the tool which looks the most promising. *Lean towards the big!* The beginner is often inclined to peck away at each area with innumerable dabs of paint. No wonder his work becomes confusing!

For skies and other large areas of tone there seldom is any reason for using small or pointed brushes. (For these areas, a knife is particularly rapid.) For linear work, on the other hand, a pointed brush (or the edge of a "flat") would be logical.

In the first minutes devoted to your underpainting, you will doubtless be working with greatly diluted paint, so choose a large brush (or a knife) so as to cover each area hastily with a washlike tone. As you later come to more and more detail you will need smaller and smaller brushes, but *always use the largest possible.*

The stiffer your paint, the slower your procedure. For outdoor work, therefore, where time is a premium, you may rightly choose to add considerable mixing medium, even at the risk of jeopardizing the permanence of your work.

We have seen that many types of subject matter suggest logical stroke directions. The ocean, to give another example, is basically level (despite its surface fluctuations), as is much meadow land. For such flat areas, strokes which are generally horizontal are customarily in order. Paradoxically, if a still body of water reveals reflections, vertical strokes may be just the thing, and meadow land, if grassy and close at hand, may also call for up-and-down strokes. We have seen that in the case of growing things—grass, shrubs, flower stalks, tree trunks, branches and the like—the strokes often follow the direction of growth. Strokes conspicuously curved should seldom be used for representing flat surfaces—walls, roofs, and beaches, etc.—but we have learned that they are ideal for expressing the three-dimensional forms of fruits, vegetables, water tanks, domes and other rounded objects. Fence boards, shingle or brick courses, masts or rigging of ships, ruts in dirt roads, formations of ledges, often give hints at logical stroke directions. And remember that strokes can sometimes effectively converge towards the perspective vanishing points. Foliage, with its multiplicity of detail, offers special problems; if near-by, it may call for strokes in many directions (suggesting the basic forms beneath), or even a dabbing or stippling of the surface. And don't forget that rough textures call for brushwork quite different from that needed by smoother ones.

Some landscape artists rely to a great extent on large strokes in the foreground, smaller ones in the middle distance, and still smaller ones in the extreme distance, perhaps arguing, subconsciously at least, that in this way they automatically gain an effect of depth and consistency of scale. Yet at times this plan may well be reversed, the extreme distance (where little detail and modeling are commonly visible) being treated with broad, inconspicuous strokes, and the middle distance with medium strokes, smaller strokes being reserved for the foreground where an increased amount of detail normally appears.

Incidentally, whenever you want a large area in your final painting (such as a sky) to look smooth and uniform, carry all of your brush strokes in one direction. The minute you change direction, the light will reveal it, as it will hit at a different angle all of the tiny ridges and grooves of which each brush stroke consists.

Backgrounds behind figures should usually be done with strokes designed to bring the figures forward, giving a sense of detachment. These strokes should not follow the contours of the figures, but should be at sharp angles to such contours.

Many of today's artists do quite a conspicuous brushwork, which means, usually, the application of paint in a heavy impasto; some make their brushwork almost a feature of their paintings. Others consider it fundamentally sounder to suppress brushwork sufficiently to prevent it from demanding the spectator's attention, unless, of course, the purpose is to create a decoration rather than a representation.

PALETTE MIXTURE VS. DIRECT APPLICATION

Another point already stressed is that it is by no means necessary to mix a hue on your palette for every area to be painted. A certain amount of mixing can be done better on your canvas. Suppose you have painted a foliage area in green. You later decided that its sunny portions should be more yellowish and the shade areas more towards the blue. Pick up some yellow on the brush—not too much thinned—and stroke it here and there on the sunny areas; it will merge in varying degrees with the green already in place. Similarly, add blue in parts of shade areas, blending it only enough to create a convincing effect. Be careful not to overblend such hues until they either lose their identity, become uninterestingly neutral, or grow muddy. And, as earlier advised, be cautious about adding white on the canvas if you would avoid an unpleasant effect. Everything depends on how you do it.

### BROKEN COLOR

In our earlier exercises we found that often, in applying paint, pleasing results are gained by dipping the brush into two or more colors at one time, conveying them directly to the canvas, where each stroke will automatically show varied blendings or minglings of the component colors. The somewhat accidental effects thus created can have great effectiveness and charm. Examine even a square inch of some portions of a painting by a professional and you are likely to find that it exhibits traces of many hues. Don't work over a given passage too long or you will lose this particular interesting variation. (It must be admitted, however, that we find some pleasing passages which have been scraped, brushed over, wiped off, and otherwise worked over repeatedly. In short, there is no fixed rule.)

### CORRECTIONS

Speaking of paint manipulation, if you are ever disappointed with the final appearance of a passage, remember that the best procedure is to scrape the paint from the entire offending area while it is still fresh and start again. And don't forget that sometimes your whole picture can advantageously be scraped, or even washed clean with a rag drenched with turpentine. Then repaint as much as seems necessary to give you the desired effect.

### FOCAL POINT

One of the frequent and conspicuous faults of paintings by beginners is that they show a scattering of interest. The eye of the spectator wanders here and there rather aimlessly, unable to discover any main idea or

*140*

*Jan De Ruth:* STUDY OF A MODEL *The rougher textures
of the background and sweater are rendered with short
bristle brushes and palette knife. The softer flesh tones are
rendered with bristle brushes, scraped and smoothed with
palette knife, and blended with softer sable brushes. The form
is further delineated with delicate strokes of the round sable.*

theme. Worse yet, some compositions show two or more features or areas of importance, each, in trying to dominate, robbing the composition of balance and unity.

What happens is this: As you work at your painting and shift your glance in order to study (and paint) one element after another throughout the entire subject, the particular element on which you focus for the moment will seem sharp and strong in relation to the rest. If, for instance, on a clear day you look at a distant mountain, you will doubtless see it in sharp detail. Yet if you paint it that way and then shift your gaze successively to the trees at the right foreground, and to the clouds above and the rocks at the left, painting each area in turn as distinctly as you see it, your finished painting may become a hodgepodge filled with too definite areas, each fighting for attention. With increased experience you will learn to play up the things which really count as you play down the rest, weaving the whole into a homogeneous composition. As a rule, the distance in particular must be lightened and simplified—made to take its place in the background, perhaps with the help of cool colors—and shadow tones throughout the picture must not be broken into sharp detail; keep them simple.

Often, as we shall see in our coming chapters on composition, you will find it wise, in such large subjects as you paint out-of-doors, to create a center of interest or focal point, exactly as in photography you would focus on the most essential elements of your subject matter. Usually (but not always) this "in focus" area will occupy the central portion of your canvas. In this area, you may well use your strongest colors, your sharpest contrasts of light and dark, your most emphatic shapes and striking elements, your greatest amount of detail. You will play down the subject matter in the corners of your picture or in the extreme distance—anything, in fact, which might tend to detract from your main idea or theme.

### REST AND THEN ANALYZE

Here is another point I wish to reiterate. Whenever you paint, in order to judge how successfully you are fulfilling your aims, turn away from your work every fifteen minutes or so. Walk around. Gaze in a new direction. Then stand far enough from your painting to see it as a whole and take an analytical look. Does some shape, some color, some detail, seem overemphatic? Then your job is to tone it down. Are your color areas well

142

distributed? Just as in a colorful fabric, you need in a painting interesting chromatic "spotting" and balance. If you think that your painting would be better with an area of blue introduced at the right, or with orange at the left, put it there whether your subject shows it or not.

### ART IS EXPERIMENTAL

In brief, never forget that you are an artist, not a color camera. I can't repeat too often that your prerogative is to be nature's master, not her slave. Nature is merely your source of inspiration—your wellspring of ideas, color schemes, subject matter of every kind. *Your job is to select, add, subtract, adjust, modify.* Keep in mind our earlier point that you don't have to be a mere reporter but rather a translator or interpreter, drawing from the visible world before you only what you wish, giving it, as you transfer it to canvas, the stamp of your own personality.

*Exercise 33: Special conditions*

To jump ahead for a minute, once you have had a fair amount of experience painting what might be called typical outdoor subjects, viewed under normal conditions, it will pay you to make experimental paintings designed to interpret not the commonplace aspects of nature but special appearances and moods. For example, go out and deliberately attempt to paint wind, sound, or odor! For at least a day, try to catch the movement of waves; on another, go after the scintillation of brilliant sunshine; on a third, the gloom of dark clouds, rain and fog, or the terror inspired by conflagration or war. Having undertaken to express the tranquility of evening, turn to such a contrasting subject as the penetrating cold and wind of a blizzard, the heat of extreme July temperature, the horizontal vastness of the prairie, the dampness of a swamp, the mystery and fearfulness of the jungle. By carrying out a definite program of this nature, you'll gain far greater stature as a painter than from any amount of "pretty picture" making.

### ADAPTATION

Eventually the time will come when you will be sufficiently familiar with nature's changing seasons and moods so that on occasion you will deliberately alter considerably the subject matter before you. In June, for instance, you may choose to paint an autumn scene, relying on your

*A. Henry Nordhausen:* RENEE *Note the free, scrubby brushwork in the background where the paint was applied thinly and semi-transparently. The direction of the strokes on the figure follow her form to emphasize the roundness. Collection, Carleton H. Palmer.*

memory for the necessary adjustments. Or perhaps the sky before you may be cloudless and you will choose to fill it with clouds. But all of this is for later. Just now you have enough with which to cope.

Don't be disappointed if you can't get—especially at first—all that you go after; at least you will gain at each trial new power and understanding. We have seen that even the long-experienced professional often fails to catch in a picture—at least at first—the thing which he most seeks. I have known a noted marine painter to admit that, in some of his early drafts of paintings, his waves have seemed frozen and static—absolutely without the desired suggestion of mobility. The same artist in another study might very successfully catch not only the feeling of water movement, but also something of its weight, its transparency—all of its liquid qualities. And so with skies. Sometimes a capable painter complains because his sky looks for a while like a stage backdrop, a flat painted curtain with clouds in fixed shapes and positions.

Obviously, to rephrase one of my thoughts above, you can't hope in your first venture into painting to master fully any one of the many essential things. Some of them no artist ever masters to his complete satisfaction; a constant challenge to improve drags him again and again to fresh effort. There is little use in my saying, "Try to paint with expression; try to capture on your canvas the mood of your subject; *try to get life and spirit into your work.*" Fundamentally, though, this is what you should do.

Although artists working in the studio from their rough sketches done out-of-doors often find it easier to gain the effects they desire than when painting in the open, frequently the opposite is true; an original sketch may possess a feeling of life and activity—real truth—which can never be recaptured later in a studio painting based upon it.

Speaking of the studio, it is of course a very common procedure for the artist to start a painting outdoors and then finish it inside. In such a case, before leaving the subject he should of course do all that he can to fix it in mind. Quick sketches or color notes should perhaps be made. Written notes of description can help, too, and sometimes snapshots from the same point of view will later prove invaluable.

### A SECOND DAY

While many outdoor paintings are completed in one sitting, *alla prima* or wet-in-wet, the artist not infrequently returns to the same scene for a second day's work. He will of course preferably choose a similar day and the same hour. If he finds that some of his color areas have in the meanwhile sunk in—dried out flat—the application of a thin coating of retouching varnish (or mixing medium) will not only restore the gloss to the surface, bringing back the proper values and hues, but it will make the surface more amenable to accept the new paint. Some artists use a fixative, not to disturb the paint configurations. While linseed oil is often substituted for retouching varnish for this coating of dried-out areas, never forget that any excess of fatty oil is undesirable. So don't keep loading on oil—or varnish, for that matter—if you are concerned with the permanency of your work.

I have heard of artists retarding drying between painting sessions by covering their paintings (and palettes) with sheets of cellulose acetate or aluminum foil to keep them from the air. When we realize that drying depends on oxidation, obviously the effectiveness of any such covering will depend on the degree to which the air is excluded. It is equally clear that such a covering must be kept from direct contact with the wet surface of a painting. Perhaps one's entire paintbox—painting, palette and all—could be slipped into an airtight bag; I haven't tried it.

### MORE ABOUT DRYING AND DRIERS

When a painting is in progress, the artist normally wants to retard its drying (unless he is building it up, layer by layer, in which case he sometimes allows each layer to dry before going on), but once it is completed he prefers to accelerate its drying process, for paintings customarily dry so slowly, even on the surface, that it is not always easy to handle or transport them.

Illustrators and other commercial artists who work in oils, and are required to meet set delivery dates, are forced to mix their paints with quick-drying varnishes or to add driers (siccatives) to their mediums. Sometimes at the end they spray a quick-drying varnish over the surface, so that this surface, at least, is dry within a matter of minutes, or, at most, in a few hours. Not only may driers be mixed with paints, but, as we saw earlier, certain paints can serve as driers. Umber, for example, contains manganese dioxide, a powerful drier, and manganese blue has a similar siccative action. If the artist wishes his work to be durable, though, he will follow our earlier advice and employ driers with caution, realizing that,

*146*

if excessively used, they may ultimately yellow, darken and crack the paint film.

As oil paint dries through oxidation, it needs lots of air, so don't leave a painting shut up in the top of your sketchbox and expect it to dry in a minimum of time. Give it air! Get it out in the open; even turn on a fan to increase air movement. As to placing paintings in the sun, there seem to be two schools of thought. Some teachers urged their students to sun their paintings; I have seen hundreds of finished canvases laid in the sun to dry just before the breaking up of a summer art school session. While this may be all right for such student work—after all, there *is* the problem of getting it home—most experts warn against putting paintings in the sun, or doing anything else, for that matter, which may interfere with the natural drying processes of fatty oils—processes so slow that it has been claimed in Max Doerner's excellent book, *The Materials of the Artist,* already mentioned, that it takes from sixty to eighty years for an oil painting to dry thoroughly! These experts point out that, in sun-dried paintings, eventual cracks are almost inevitable; also, the canvas, frame and panel all contract with possible detrimental results. (Paintings need light, on the other hand; they yellow if faced to the wall, and many an artist has bleached his work, reducing the yellow to some extent, by placing it in the sun. So there you are!)

The best drier is said to be cobalt linoleate. This is a so-called "top drier," working from without. Various others are on the market. Usually they come in liquid form. Only a tiny amount is ever needed, not over two percent of the painting medium—in other words, a few drops. Driers accomplish their job by promoting the absorption of oxygen by the paint film. Thin paint applications containing driers usually dry thoroughly in a few hours. In the case of thick applications—impasto—a top drier will accomplish little beyond causing a tough film to form on the surface; this will actually prevent the air from reaching the underlying layers, and so will retard drying within. So paintings, bone dry to the touch, can easily fool you.

TRANSPORTATION

Whether you use driers or not, don't cut canvas from your stretcher frames and roll it, as I have known students to do. I remember that one student, on going home after a summer school session, wrongly assumed that his paintings were dry, so he rolled a dozen or more together. When later he tried to unroll this work he found it cemented into a solid mass, paintings and canvas ruined. Even if paintings are dry, rolling will crack the paint films, so *never roll*. (If it should sometimes prove absolutely necessary to roll canvas, roll it *face out* around as large a cylinder as is available.) And it is scarcely safer to stack such paintings, whether with or without some such thing as cellophane between. Never use newspaper or other printed material in contact with painted canvas. Not only is the paper almost certain to stick, but the printer's ink will often transfer to the painted surfaces.

For transporting paintings done on panels, it is easy to build a case on the order of that in Figure 43, provided with the desired number of

Detail of grooves

Sides of thin plywood

*Figure 43*

SHIPPING CASE *Eight panels can be shipped in this case, two to each groove, back to back. Thus paintings not yet dry can easily be transported without injury.*

separated grooves or slots into which the paintings can be fitted securely. If such a case is to be shipped, the open end need not be covered with wood; it may be stuffed full of crumpled newspapers and the whole then enclosed in wrapping paper. If used as a carrying case, rather than a shipping case, a wooden end can be hinged to serve as a cover; a handle can easily be attached.

### DON'T DESTROY

No matter how disappointing a painting may prove when completed, don't throw it away in disgust. Lay it to one side for a while. Forget it entirely. Then look at it some day with a fresh eye; you will more than likely now see possibilities in it. If not, you know that as a last resort you can paint the whole thing over. Probably far less drastic treatment will be called for, however.

### FINAL VARNISHING

Almost any oil painting, after it has dried for a while, loses its initial gloss and becomes dull, at least in some areas. It looks flat and dead. At such a time it is customary to give it a thin coat (or two) of picture varnish. This will both improve its appearance and protect it from dust, dirt, dampness and any harmful gases in the atmosphere.

This varnishing should be delayed for a considerable period—two or three months to a year after a painting is finished. Above all, the painting must not anywhere be sticky to the touch. The varnishing should be done in a moderately warm room, and the picture should be at room temperature; the varnish can be warmer but not hot. *The picture must be absolutely dry,* for if dampness is present a troublesome and unsightly "bloom," "bluing," or fogginess may develop. Therefore, don't varnish on humid, muggy days. All dust must previously be whisked away with a soft, dry cloth or brush and, during the varnishing process and while drying, the varnish must be kept free from dust. There may be some air motion but direct drafts should be avoided.

Some experts, in order to obtain a thin and uniform coat of varnish, spray it on with a mechanical airbrush, but most artists use a regular varnish brush an inch or more wide (avoid one which sheds its hair), applying the varnish thinly and lightly. The picture is usually laid almost flat on a table, pitched just enough to aid the artist, who, starting at the top, works gradually to the bottom, making certain to touch every spot, for it might show if he were to go back into it after it starts to set. If varnish is too thick, laps may show, so test it before you use it. Some recommend the immediate rebrushing of the whole varnished area (before it starts to set) as a means of spreading the varnish uniformly, overcoming laps or like effects. Without adding any new varnish it can be brushed in two or three directions.

As to kind of varnish for this final work, it is claimed that the resin varnishes are much to be preferred to the fatty oils. Pure damar (the first choice of many) or mastic varnishes dry out within a day (especially the ethereal type), while oily varnishes such as copal may remain sticky for months. Mastic and damar cooked in oil are unsuitable. Avoid also for final varnishing the so-called retouching varnishes, asking your dealer for "final picture" varnish containing no oil. Spirit varnish should never be used; it becomes hard and brittle. Varnish should always be new and fresh, by the way, as all varnishes deteriorate with age no matter how tightly bottled.

### REPAINTING DISCARDED CANVASES

An old worthless painting, unless badly damaged, can be repainted with another subject, whatever its age. If such a painting has been but thinly executed so that it doesn't show heavy brush or knife strokes, it should first be rubbed with a mild solvent to remove any surface oil. Retouching varnish should then be applied, after which an entirely new white lead ground can be put on with a palette knife. Such a ground, by the way, can be textured to suit by working it (while it is still soft) with brushes of different kinds. It should be allowed to dry at least a week before working upon it.

If an old painting shows a heavy impasto, the excess roughness must first be removed with medium sandpaper, after which the retouching varnish is applied and the process continued as described in the previous paragraph.

The experts don't all approve of such repainting; some of them point to the possible later difficulties caused by the previously applied paint gradually "bleeding" through to show, but many a canvas has been reclaimed in this manner to last for years and years.

One can even use the back side of an old canvas. Restretch the canvas on the frame, reversed. Then make a "size" by dissolving common household gelatin in hot water in the proportion of three-quarters of an ounce of gelatin to one pint of water. When the jellied substance has cooled, spread it thinly and evenly over the canvas with your palette knife, working it into the fabric thoroughly. When it has solidified—as it will in a few hours—apply a white lead ground. For this, commercial white lead oil paste will do, thinned if necessary with retouching varnish, sparingly used. (White lead and zinc, half and half, will make a still better ground.) Spread the lead all over the canvas with your palette knife, forcing it from all angles with considerable pressure. Scrape off any surplus; then let it dry for a week or so. If necessary, add a second coat; seldom will this be needed.

*150*

# Chapter 15

## GLAZES, SCUMBLES AND SUCH

BEFORE TURNING TO the all-important matter of pictorial composition, it seems well to round out our exposition of painting procedures by a brief reference to certain pertinent technical matters not yet touched upon.

Much of our discussion to this point has related to the common practice of today of painting in oils very directly *(alla prima)*, finishing a picture at one sitting or, at the most, in two or three.

We have seen that, following this method, the artist usually first outlines his subject on a suitable ground in pencil or charcoal. He then "fixes" this, or dusts it off until it is barely visible. Next he perfects his outline in thinned paint—French ultramarine, burnt umber, whatever suits his fancy; he may even start with this paint instead of pencil or charcoal. There are now several directions he may take: 1. He may paint the dark portions of his subject quickly, freely, sketchily, using the same color just used for layout, often greatly thinned with turpentine, sometimes mixed with white; frequently he retains unpainted canvas areas for his lights. 2. Instead, he may coat his entire canvas with a thin underpainting in colors approximating those of his subject. 3. He may make this underpainting in colors complementary to those of his subject. Whichever procedure he follows, he will keep his paint thin; if superfluous paint starts to pile up he will scrape it off. To this point he may treat all areas simply and flatly, with modeling scarcely more than indicated.

*151*

With underpainting completed, there will come a checking up, followed by a repainting or refining of incorrect proportions. If this work should run into a second day, he will start this second day's work by covering with retouch varnish or medium any areas which have dried flat. Now will follow work with somewhat thicker paint—a gradual building up of the whole painting, area by area. Proportions will be further refined; modeling will be advanced; the best possible adjustment of colors will be worked out. Now less turpentine or other thinner will be used, but mediums richer in oils will be substituted.

Eventually, still thicker paint (fresh from the tube, perhaps) will be employed preferably in strokes here and there, not uniformly all over. We know, though, that if we pile great blobs of color over continuous thick, pasty undercoats, the results will be far from permanent. (Heavy impasto strokes may prove quite durable if broken or scattered.) Therefore, at no time will we use more paint than needed.

By all such means, overconspicuous passages will gradually be simplified—toned down—and meager passages will be strengthened. Detail will be added, and, at last, the finishing touches, particularly the highlights, will be put in place.

### GLAZES

In contrast to the above direct or *alla prima* procedures—stressed throughout this book—there is another method of oil painting which has long had considerable following (the old masters, particularly the Venetians, used it frequently)—a method employing thin coats of paint (mixtures of transparent paints and mediums) known as glazes. Normally these glazes are applied over dried underpaintings done in oil paint or tempera (the latter not our consideration here). They make possible an optical result quite unlike that considered to this point, for the color of the underpainting merges or blends with that of each glaze.

Sometimes an entire painting is done with glazes; again, they are used only on limited areas. Special glazing mediums are available. A useful one consists of half and half of stand oil and damar varnish (heavy). A little turpentine can be added, as well as a bit of cobalt drier.

The transparent colors which are bright and clear in hue, with strong tinting power, are the best for glazing. Often they are mixed in saucers to a syrupy or varnish-like consistency. Among the oil colors which are

*152*

sufficiently transparent to lend themselves well to glazing—though these vary in different makes—are ultramarine, alizarin crimson, burnt sienna and viridian green. Semitransparent are cadmium red and yellow, Prussian blue and yellow ochre. Varying degrees of opacity will be found in white lead, cerulean blue, umber, Naples yellow, Venetian red and ivory black. One can of course test one's own paints for transparency.

Obviously, when transparent glazes are to be used, the color of the underpainting must be considered with care. Also, the underpainting should be thoroughly dry before glazes are added. (To many artists, the term "underpainting" always suggests a dry foundation, never a wet one.) Just before the glaze is applied, the underpainting should be *slightly* moistened with the painting medium. The glazing may be done with a painting brush, a soft brush known as a blender, or a pad or dauber of cheesecloth. The dauber, lightly loaded with paint, is tapped, pounced or stroked onto the underpainting. Edges are best glazed by the careful use of fine brushes. Blendings between two superimposed glaze colors are usually done before the first has set, the two wet colors being worked into each other.

### IMPRIMATURA OR TONED GROUND

A glaze on a white ground is sometimes called an imprimatura. As a rule, such a glaze is transparent. A toned ground, on the contrary, is an opaque solid color executed on the white canvas. Often such a ground, of any suitable tone, is prepared far enough in advance so it can become a well-dried foundation for the work in glaze to follow. In short, a toned ground is, in effect, merely a very opaque kind of underpainting. Such a ground can be applied to the canvas quickly, thinly and evenly through the use of a palette or painting knife. When one plans to paint on such a ground, the drawing is made directly upon the ground (or is transferred to it). For, if done upon the canvas, it would be obliterated by the opaque ground when later applied.

### SCUMBLES

This is another somewhat vague term which commonly refers to the daubing of an entire painting (or some large area of it) with a thin coating of color—usually, but not always, opaque—mixed with any desired thinner.

*153*

Scumble may be done over paint which is dry to the touch or has been isolated with a coat of varnish. Sometimes the paint used for scumbling, having been brushed on, is partly wiped off with a rag, leaving a uniform coating of the desired tone. Or it may be rubbed on with a brush, rag or the finger; occasionally it is stippled. In general, scumbling has a softening effect. Often it is resorted to as a corrective method wherever a tone seems too obtrusive, perhaps because of overworked detail which can, through scumbling, be successfully veiled.

We have touched but briefly—and very inadequately—on these matters. The reader interested in pursuing them further—and other so-called "mixed" techniques, some of them involving tempera, casein, etc.—should consult some of the technical treatises of the type listed on page 19.

*Exercise 34: Glazes and scumbles*
Sooner or later, why not investigate and experiment with some of these things, thus broadening your technical know-how?

*Chapter 16*

PICTORIAL COMPOSITION

FROM THE VERY START of your painting career, there's one problem that will constantly force itself on your attention. This is the all-important problem of how to "compose" each picture. A painting may be good as to subject matter, drawing, color, and technique, but if its component parts are poorly organized—poorly adjusted one to another—it will nevertheless be a failure. So let's take a look at some basic principles and practices of the vital art of pictorial composition.

### CREATING A PICTURE

We have repeatedly seen that many beginning artists, when they first turn to the painting of pictures, are under the mistaken impression that in nature they will find an inexhaustible supply of ready-made subjects just waiting to be transferred "as is" to their canvas. We have pointed out that this is not so—that only occasionally will one be so lucky as to come across a subject which, if it is to result in an esthetically satisfying painting, will not have to be altered in many respects during the process of its pictorial development.

Nature, in other words, furnishes an overabundance—often a confusion—of pictorial ingredients from which the artist gradually learns to select for any given painting only those relevant to his immediate purpose. These he arranges and rearranges, emphasizing some and subordinating others, altering sizes and shapes, developing effective contrasts of light and dark, adjusting color relationships, perhaps adding elements of his own or substituting one element for another, until at last he achieves a reasonably pleasing pictorial result which sometimes bears but little resemblance to its original source.

Stated differently, instead of being a mere recorder or reporter of some of nature's lavish offerings, making it his main business to try to transfer them to canvas as faithfully as he can in a sort of photographic fashion, the artist, having discriminatingly selected a limited area of subject matter or a controlled number of objects, becomes a skillful adjuster, improvisor and inventor—in brief, something of a creator. His normal aim is to make of each finished painting a satisfying composition—one capable of stirring, and usually of pleasing, his fellow man.

How does the artist accomplish all this? Are there rules to guide him—recipes as specific as we find in music? Unfortunately, no: one cannot learn to paint by recipe; let me emphasize once again that one must learn largely through trial and error. In fact, many successful paintings defy analysis; it is hard to say why they affect us as they do; sometimes they even go contrary to established and generally approved procedures.

There are, however, certain basic principles and practices of the art of pictorial composition which are well within the grasp of the beginning student, and which can prove decidedly helpful as a guide to his effort, a test of his accomplishment to any given point, and a sort of springboard from which he may jump in any desired corrective direction. A working knowledge of even these few things, if conscientiously applied to your everyday efforts, will help you to choose a good subject, to view it from the ideal position, to rearrange its elements, to translate it effectively as you carry it to canvas.

As a preface to our discussion, let me remind you that in composition there may well be fundamental differences of approach, according to whether one works from relatively small subjects (often indoors) such as still life, flowers, or posed figures, or has chosen the wide open spaces. In the former case, the artist will probably do much of his composing long before he puts brush to canvas. Take still life, for example. First of all, he is practically certain to select individual items which he believes can be grouped harmoniously—their choice is his own. Then, utilizing such general principles of composition as are offered below, he will experiment with these items in all sorts of arrangements, perhaps substituting one object for another, until at last he creates a setup which pleases him because of its successful disposition of shapes, tones, colors, patterns and textures. (Incidentally, here's a reminder that his view finder will prove useful in this connection.) In other words, he will pose his material much as a photographer would. Lighting is especially important; sometimes it takes a half-hour just to hit on the most effective amount, quality, and direction of illumination. When his setup is finally ready, his job is half-done—the actual painting on canvas will be vastly aided by all this careful preliminary preparation. His creative effort largely behind him, he can now be a sort of color camera, though constant readjustments and refinements will be necessary as his painting proceeds.

If, on the other hand, he paints outdoors, much of his composition may have to be worked on his canvas, or by means of preliminary studies in some such medium as pencil, charcoal, or pastel, for obviously he will seldom have the privilege of rearranging his actual subject matter to suit his taste. He can't, for instance, transplant living trees or shift buildings at will, nor can he control the light, which will constantly alter in direction and intensity as the hours go by.

Sometimes disconcerting things happen to outdoor subjects: One starts to paint a shore scene, and a boat—the main object of attention —sails away. Or the tide goes out, substituting unsightly mud flats for the clear water with its crystal reflections. Clouds or fogs appear, obscuring the sun or veiling the landscape. The cows wander off or the farmer draws away the haystacks. Therefore, even if the artist tries to choose an outdoor subject which promises to give a reasonably satisfactory pictorial effect, at least for a few hours, he knows in advance that at best he may need to do a lot of recomposing as he goes along, either directly on his canvas or by means of such supplementary studies as have just been mentioned.

In this connection, I might profitably call attention once again to a point made in an earlier chapter: that, because of nature's complexities of subject matter, on the one hand, and the ephemeral quality of her effects, on the other, many professional painters, including some world-renowned masters, never do anything in the open but quick studies and written notes—just enough to prompt their memories as they create their finished paintings in the calm and quiet of their studios.

But enough by way of preamble. Let's get on to our basic principles of composition and their practical application—principles and procedures which apply whether one works indoors or out, and regardless of subject matter, painting medium, or method.

First, what is this thing called composition? Webster defines it as: "Formation of a whole or integral by placing together different things, parts or ingredients . . . manner of being composed as to style or elements . . . state or quality of being put together . . . conjunction; combination; adjustment . . . the art or practice of so combining the parts of a work of art as to produce a harmonious whole . . . result of composing; that which is composed or has been composed."

The word composition therefore normally implies the availability of more than one thing or part to compose. If—to take a simple example—we have an object such as a tree (A, Figure 44), and another object

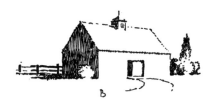

A          B          C

*The elements of a composition.*

*Figure 44*
**COMPOSITION** *This demonstrates that composition is the art of putting together various elements to form a unified whole, each part adjusted to all other parts.*

D

*The elements combined.*

E

*Another simple arrangement.*

such as a barn (B), and still another object such as a clump of bushes (C), we possess the ingredients needed for an elementary composition. Our job is to compose or arrange these ingredients into a satisfactory picture. This can often be done in a number of ways even without changing shapes and sizes—see (D) and (E) for typical and self-explanatory solutions. If we wish to change shapes and sizes (or add other elements) the possibilities are almost unlimited.

UNITY

In any such problems, regardless of subject matter, the artist must make sure that he includes nothing or does nothing which will cloud or obscure his main intent.

This means that he must observe the principle of unity, *which requires that a composition be a homogeneous whole, all of its parts related and so merged or blended that they express one main thought.* In order to secure unity in painting, one should select only as much of the material before him as relates directly to the subject of his picture. He should separate his subject from everything else that is visible and then think of it as a single harmonious whole. This rule applies whether the subject be a group of still life, a portion of a photograph, or something else.

To illustrate this principle of unity, let us turn to still life and consider some simple objects found in everyday use. An ink bottle, a turnip, and a vase of roses might perhaps be arranged into a pleasing composition so far as form, size, value, and color are concerned, but to some degree unity would always be lacking in such a group, for these objects are not sufficiently well related by use ever to become a satisfying whole. It would be equally difficult to compose a coal scuttle, a hair brush, and a glass pitcher, but a comparatively simple matter to form an excellent composition of a loaf of bread partly sliced, with knife, plate of cheese, napkin, etc., or a garden trowel, flowerpot and package of seeds. (Remember that these are all general principles, subject to exception. Many extremely satisfactory paintings to some degree go contrary to them.) When it comes to such larger subjects as buildings with their landscape settings, or ships at sea or shore, little difficulty is likely to be experienced in choosing objects which go well together. Unity by no means depends on selection alone, however, as we shall discover.

(Whenever you have a painting under way, check to see if it possesses this quality of unity.)

This brings us to a second principle—that of balance; this is so closely related to the principle of unity as to be really a part of it. In fact, without balance there could be no unity, for *by balance we mean, as the name implies, the equilibrium or restfulness that results from having all the parts of a composition so arranged and so emphasized or subordinated that each receives just its correct share of attention.* Every part of a picture has a certain attractive force which acts upon the eye; and, in proportion to this power, it detracts from every other part. If we find our interest divided definitely between several parts—if certain tones or colors seem too insistent or prominent—we know that the composition is lacking in balance.

It is impossible to give rules for obtaining balance in pictures, mainly for the reason that the attractive force of each portion depends on an infinite number of factors which are variable. A short, straight line painted near the center of a clean canvas has a power to catch and hold the eye. But let a figure 7 or some zigzag line be painted near the straight one and, even though they are of equal size, the zigzag line will usually prove the more powerful attraction of the two. In the same way, a star-shaped form or a triangle has more tendency to draw attention than a square or rectangle of like area. Ability to attract depends not entirely on shape, however, but likewise on values of light and dark. Paint two squares side by side, one dark and the other light, and if the canvas is white the dark square will exert the strongest force, but if the canvas is dark the white square will jump into prominence. Also, power to attract depends on color. Readers don't need to be told that a bright color, especially in a large area, catches the eye much more quickly than a dull color of like area. Again, the attractive power of an object varies in proportion to its proximity to other objects. If, for example, a man is shown at small scale standing or sitting near the center of a comparatively blank canvas, he will receive considerable attention, but if surrounded by other objects he will seem much less noticeable. Similarly, animate objects as a rule demand more attention than inanimate objects of like size. Then, too, a moving object, or one which suggests motion, will be more prominent than a similar object in repose. (A running man will usually be seen far more quickly than one at rest.) Objects near the edges or corners of the canvas usually arrest the eye more quickly, too, than if nearer the center, though much depends on circumstances.

(As balance in a painting changes slightly with every brush stroke you make, test each painting repeatedly as you proceed in order to judge whether it is "out of balance" or "in balance.")

### EMPHASIS AND SUBORDINATION

If you minutely examine any object in nature, you will see an overwhelming mass of small detail. Even as you sit in a room and glance about, you will find, if you search, thousands of spots of color or of light and shade. These tiny spots are of many kinds, including the lines of the delicate graining of the wood, the hundreds of partly visible threads from which the hangings and upholstery materials are woven, and the myriad indentations and projections of the masonry and plaster. It is hardly necessary to point out that even if it were desirable it would be impossible to indicate each of these spots correctly on a canvas of average size. Instead, if the artist wished to depict the room he would try to represent the effect of the whole, the effect that he gets not when he hunts for such details but when he enters the room and glances around in the usual way. If for an instant he focuses his attention on a single object such as a chair in a room corner, he sees little detail excepting in the chair itself and in those objects adjacent to it, for his eyes, when on that area, are not clearly focused on other things. Even in that area one is not conscious of each tiny spot, but instead notices the general impression of color and tone. The chair, being directly in the range of vision, is for the moment the center of interest, and the other objects become more and more blurred the farther they are from this center, unless, of course, the eye is turned.

It really is surprising what a relatively small area we are able to see plainly when our eyes are thus focused in one fixed direction. We are so accustomed to shifting our eyes constantly from one object to another that we may fail to realize this limitation. Stand within ten feet of a door and gaze intently at the knob. Without shifting the eyes, are you able to see the top of the door distinctly? If you raise your eyes and look at the top, do you see the bottom plainly? Go to the window and look at some building across the street. Fix your sight on an upper window, the chimney or some point on the roof. Are not the lower portions of the building blurred and indistinct unless you shift your gaze to them? When you look at the foundation you do not see the roof distinctly.

*161*

Now in painting actual things or places it is often—though not always—assumed that the artist is recording but one moment of time, while looking mainly in one fixed direction. He gazes at some interesting object, or, if the object is too large to come entirely within his range of vision, he selects some prominent feature. Then the object as a whole, or the feature, becomes the point of focus (center of interest), just as when one is using the camera focused on some particular area. As we saw in an earlier chapter, in making a painting this same natural scheme is often carried out; the strongest contrasts and the sharpest details are developed at this center of interest, the work growing less and less distinct towards the edges of the canvas. Almost all paintings which are imitative of nature, such as those of landscapes, street scenes, buildings, etc., can advantageously have the center of interest thus emphasized (though not overemphasized) with everything else nicely subordinated. *Above all, one must not have in a painting two or more centers showing equal emphasis,* for in such case they will constantly fight for attention. Sometimes the objects painted are small enough, or at sufficient distance, so that the entire subject as contained within the canvas area becomes the center of interest. This is often true of still-life groups.

The artist has an amazing degree of control in this matter. He can draw the spectator's attention to almost any part of his picture. The accompanying illustrations (Figures 45 and 46) demonstrate in a somewhat exaggerated manner one way in which the artist can lead the spectator's eye more or less at will to a focal point of any desired part of a composition. In Figure 45, the focal point is obviously low; in Figure 46

*Figure 45*
**CENTER OF INTEREST** *Here the eye is focused around the lower archway. (Compare with Figure 46.)*

*Figure 46*
CENTER OF INTEREST *The eye has been raised to the upper archway. This becomes the area of focus.*

it is high. In both cases, the control resulted almost wholly from creating strong value contrasts and sharp edges where the focal point was to be developed. By strengthening contrasts of hue in such areas, even more dramatic effects are possible.

In discussing balance we mentioned certain ways of obtaining emphasis wherever wanted. To state them differently, in creating most paintings the artist relies for emphasis (1) on the character of his subject matter; (2) on bright color (or strong contrasts of color); (3) on very light or very dark values (or strong contrasts of value); (4) on line (perhaps outline brushed around a leading object); (5) on unusual shapes; (6) on things in abnormal positions; (7) on noticeable textures or techniques (such as palette knife work or heavy brush strokes); (8) on exaggerated depiction of details; (9) on the use of animate or moving objects.

The beginner sometimes finds it hard to omit elements—particularly details—which are irrelevant or distracting. This is because he sees them plainly in his subject matter. Yet to obtain a successful result he should omit them, or at least subordinate them. The latter he does in just the opposite way from obtaining emphasis; i.e., in painting these elements he avoids the strong colors, sharp tonal contrasts, definite linear work, conspicuous textures and other attention-demanding factors just mentioned. In this connection, let me advise you again that if a given passage in painting becomes too persistent, you should scrape it lightly with your

*163*

palette knife, blur it with a soft brush (blender), rub thumb or finger through it; overpaint (scumble) it with a thin veil of inconspicuous color; or break it up with dabs of your brush, with or without color.

(Repeatedly as a painting progresses, test it with these thoughts in mind. Hunt for things both large and small which you might think better be emphasized, subordinated or omitted.)

### CONSISTENCY VS. INCONSISTENCY

From all of this, it should be plain that the more consistent one's handling throughout a painting—one's brush strokes and one's use of line, tone and color—the greater will be its unity. Some paintings are entirely lacking in unity and tend to "fly to pieces" because one area shows one sort of handling, a second area another, and perhaps a third area still a third. The beginner is usually wise, therefore, not to exhibit too many handlings in any one painting. As he becomes more expert, he may now and then be deliberately inconsistent in order to stress certain of his passages—usually those at or about his center of interest. His inconsistencies may range from very mild ones to very evident ones, and they may take any of a number of forms, including those referred to as valuable for obtaining emphasis. He may, for example, use more vigorous brushwork in these passages than in the remainder of the painting, or even resort to his palette knife for applying paint. He may utilize abnormally bright colors, sometimes going so far as to choose inharmonious color in order to emphasize a point. He may introduce some surprising element of subject matter—something so incongruous as to attract attention.

While such planned inconsistencies, under proper control, can occasionally serve a useful purpose, there is another type of inconsistency which can lead to absurd results. When the artist in his studio develops a painting based on sketches made outdoors, aided perhaps by snapshots, mental notes, and the like, he can easily fall into inconsistencies which are inexcusable. He may, for instance, borrow a building from one sketch and another building from a second sketch, combining them in his painting. Unless he is a master of perspective, these two buildings, originally seen from different points of view—perhaps one from above and the other from below, or one from near-by and the other from the distance—may show perspective inconsistencies disturbing to even the relatively untutored spectator (though he may not understand exactly what is wrong). Inconsistencies of lighting are also common. An old barn may be painted with the light from the left, and a tree or cloud, brought into the composition from another source, may be lighted from the right! Figures or animals may be too large or too small in relation to their surroundings (a characteristic of the work of the "primitive" painter). All of which points to the fact that one should possess more than a modicum of knowledge before he can hope with any great degree of success to combine in an original composition elements from unrelated sources.

### SOME ADDITIONAL FACTORS

In books on pictorial composition, you will find discussions not only of such matters as we have dealt with here, but of such other factors as rhythm, progression, opposition or contrast, transition, repetition, alternation, functionalism, etc. If you wish to investigate all these things, we suggest that you refer to some of the standard books.

# Chapter 17

## COMPOSITION
## DEMONSTRATED

IT'S ALL very well to talk about such things as unity, balance, emphasis, and subordination, but many of these are but words until the artist actually starts to make a picture. Then he usually begins to see that mere words can prove very helpful—can even provide quite a definite guide to his procedure. For one thing, they start him thinking so that, instead of blindly sailing into his first attempts at picture making, hoping that luck will see him successfully through, he *plans* each picture intelligently.

You are going out with me now as I prepare to paint an actual picture. But before we leave home, let's briefly review some of the ground we have already repeatedly been over.

First, we have reiterated again and again that the artist interested in representational (naturalistic) painting is seldom satisfied to transfer to his canvas as literally as possible (much as a camera might do) some small section of nature. Often his subject is too large and needs great reduction or it is too complex and requires simplification. Again, its elements are individually interesting but nature has arranged them in a manner which will not prove esthetically effective when recorded on canvas. Therefore, the artist selects only those elements before him which at the moment have a strong appeal and seem relevant to his purposes; these he arranges and rearranges, adjusting them in size, shape, tone, color, and relationship one to another until at last he obtains an effect which, realistic though it may be in general appearance, is nevertheless to a considerable measure the product of his own creative faculties.

To some extent, the artist is much like the musician who, in composing music, almost never copies the precise sounds of birds, animals, people, the wind, the waves, thunder, and all the other myriad things in nature. (It would never occur to most people, in fact, that the composer *should* so imitate nature's sounds, though many of these same people inconsistently seem to think that the painter should imitate every detail of her appearances.) Instead, the musician, starting to compose, selects from all the sounds which exist only a few which are related and are capable of being reproduced on available musical instruments. These sounds he arranges and rearranges again and again, emphasizing some and subordinating others, experimenting, changing, substituting one for another, until at last he develops a unified composition scarcely more than reminiscent of nature but bearing the imprint of his own personality.

The painter follows much the same basic procedure. As seen in earlier chapters, there are various ways in which he experiments with his pictorial elements in order to compose them into a unified whole. If sufficiently experienced, he may be able to make most of his vital adjustments of form mentally during the process of sketching his subject matter on his canvas. He enlarges one feature to give it emphasis. He shrinks another. Something incongruous or nonessential he omits. If, in his subject matter, certain perspective convergences seem too acute or some areas of foreshortening too extreme, he modifies them without hesitation.

What guides him in this? It is hard to say. As in many other things in life, a sort of inner voice or disciplined instinct tells him what to do. He reasons—yes. But he is hardly aware of his reasoning; his adjustments are usually made almost subconsciously.

With his proportions established on his canvas, he continues to make adjustments as he goes on to his work in tone and color, often doing so with an amazing facility and sensitivity born of long practice. If all goes well, in an hour or two—or in a day or two; there can be no rule—he brings to completion a satisfying result, convincingly real yet often surprisingly different from the scene before him.

Some other painters—even men of enviable capacity and reputation —never develop this sureness and swiftness. They seem to blunder and fumble, buried in doubt, hesitatingly trying this and that, perhaps becoming discouraged and abandoning the project for a time. Yet in the end they may come through with a praiseworthy—even a triumphant—result.

In other words, art is art and not science. This is one reason why it is hard to learn, hard to teach, and hard to do.

### PRELIMINARY STUDIES, MEDIUM AND TYPE

May I again remind the beginner—who is all too often impatient to rush his work to a quick finish—that many experienced artists never go onto their final canvas until they have made a number of trial studies. For the student or beginning amateur this practice is almost a necessity. Some painters produce these on scraps of canvas in full oil colors, so complete and so carefully adjusted that their virtues are comparable to those of the much larger final paintings based upon them. Other preliminary studies are crude and to the casual observer almost meaningless; their making aids the artist, however, to form a clear mental plan of the work to follow.

Not all artists paint or draw such studies—whether thumbnail or larger sketches—in color but in black and white, favorite mediums being wash (monochrome watercolor), charcoal, and pencil. Some artists are forever producing such studies, not only when they plan to turn at once to painting the same subject, but whenever they find an opportunity. Often they do this work in notebooks or sketchbooks and save it—an excellent idea, for many a crude sketch which seems practically valueless when made, later becomes the source of a fine painting.

### PROPORTION OF PRELIMINARIES

Regardless of medium, it makes sense to follow the plan earlier suggested to draw preliminary sketches to the approximate proportion visualized for the final painting. If a painting is to measure 16 x 20 inches, for example, each preliminary might measure 2 x 2½ inches, or 4 x 5 inches.

### TRACING PAPER

More and more artists have in recent years discovered in tracing paper —formerly used almost exclusively by architects and engineers—an ideal

*Allen Glicksman:* BLUE VASE  *This composition has been
very carefully arranged. The lines of the ladder and red
drapery lead upward to the vase of flowers, the focal point
in the picture. The vase is framed by the drapery
and edge of the picture behind. Notice how the form of
the vase is echoed by the image in the picture behind.*

material for studies in pencil or charcoal. It comes in rolls, sheets, or pads; the latter form is best for most small studies. Be sure to buy a type which is reasonably transparent.

### BY WAY OF ILLUSTRATION

We show by the reproductions offered as Figures 47-51 a typical use of tracing paper.

I was driving along the Maine coast one day and came to a neighborhood filled with interesting subject matter. Leaving my car, I wandered along a rocky path, my only sketching materials a pad of tracing paper and a soft (4B) pencil. Soon I came to a subject which appealed to me. This I quickly recorded (Figure 47), following nature's proportions very closely. (This drawing was 8½ inches wide.)

*Figure 47*
**THE FIRST SKETCH**  *These pencil sketches show how tracing paper can be used to improve composition. This first sketch followed nature's proportions very closely.*

I of course realized that, although such a long composition is suitable for drawing, it is not well adapted to the proportions of the typical canvas. Therefore, another sheet of tracing paper was immediately placed over this and a second sketch (Figure 48) was made with the tree at the left moved much closer to the fishing shack. The horizontal dimension

*Figure 48*
**THE SECOND SKETCH**  *Here individual elements were traced in a fresh relationship to shorten the rectangle.*

was still too great and I wished to experiment further with the composition, so in a third sketch (Figure 49) even more freedom was used. The tree was moved to the extreme right and only a portion of the building

*Figure 49*
**THE THIRD SKETCH**
*Additional elements were introduced and the whole brought to canvas proportion.*

was pictured at the left. Although with further study this sketch could be made the basis of a successful painting, the large dark masses seemed somewhat scattered, so a new sketch (Figure 50) was at once drawn directly on top of the previous one. This gives us a leading dark area at

*Figure 50*
**THE FOURTH SKETCH**
*Here is still another study using artistic license. Many such sketches are often needed.*

the left and bottom. (Incidentally, the net reel and figures here are too small in relation to the building.)

Lacking time and equipment to do my painting at the site, I started back to my car with the feeling that my last sketch would serve as a satisfactory guide for a later studio painting. But half a mile down the

*171*

*Figure 51*
THE FIFTH SKETCH *The actual painting was based on this different, though similar, subject.*

road I came upon another group of buildings and quickly blocked out the sketch shown as Figure 51. This sketch I have actually used a half-dozen times since, not only for an oil painting but, with variations, for several watercolors and a pen sketch or two. The sketch in Figure 50 is still held with a future painting in mind. (These last sketches were all about 6 or 6½ inches in width.)

### PENCIL VS. CHARCOAL

In some ways, charcoal—especially the softer, less brittle type—is more desirable than pencil for such preliminaries, for charcoal lends itself rather better to tonal work, giving soft, deep values not unlike those produced with oil paints. The pencil, with its greater ability to hold a sharp point, is indisputedly supreme for linear treatments, and it smudges somewhat less easily, so has its place in the artist's kit. Don't forget that a spray of fixative will hold either pencil or charcoal in place, preventing smudging.

### PASTELS, COLORED CRAYONS, AND PENCILS

All the above sketches were in black and white only. I felt that the appeal of the subject matter in this instance depended little on color, so once the sketch, Figure 51, had been blocked out on the canvas (not reproduced here), the color scheme was kept very close to nature, which served as a satisfactory guide.

Some subjects intrigue the artist mainly because of their color, in which case any black-and-white preliminary study seems wholly inadequate. For such subjects, oils, watercolors, pastels, or other forms of colored crayons or pencils are preferable. Pastels don't hold their points well, though, having much the friability of charcoal. So when using either pastels or charcoal it is generally better to work at larger scale than when using pencils (whether black or colored) having firmer points.

### TRANSFERRING TO CANVAS

When a subject has been quite accurately delineated in a thumbnail sketch, it can easily be transferred to the canvas in the same proportion. A common method is indicated by Figure 51—a method used by artists since the earliest times. This sketch, on completion, was ruled off into squares. A canvas of the same proportions was similarly ruled off in the same number of correspondingly larger squares. It was then comparatively simple to copy in each large square on the canvas the contents of the corresponding small one on the sketch. After this, a bit of refining was all that was necessary before the painting was begun.

### ENLARGING APPARATUS

Probably most readers are familiar with such common devices for enlargement as the pantograph, projector, and proportional dividers. Through the use of one of these it is quite easy for anyone to "blow up" a small sketch (or photograph) to larger proportions of any reasonable dimensions.

In the case of the pantograph, the artist merely guides a pointed tool with which he carefully traces each major line of his sketch. Another point simultaneously and automatically reproduces on the canvas, properly enlarged, every outline which the operator traces.

The projector, by means of light, reflects an entire small sketch, print, or photo—not merely the outline, but color and values—directly onto the canvas, where the artist traces as much of the projected image as he desires. Slide projectors are also used, the subject on a photographic slide being thrown, greatly enlarged, onto the artist's canvas. The canvas serves as a screen on which the artist traces the projected image. Thus one with little skill in drawing can outline on his canvas even the most difficult subjects, such as faces or figures.

Another instrument often used in enlarging is known as "proportional dividers." The artist sets these dividers by scale to any desired degree of enlargement. Then, one at a time, he measures the salient dimension of the sketch, transferring each in turn to the canvas.

*Exercise 35: Sketching, enlarging*
You would do well to play around for a while with a variety of such sketching materials as we have mentioned, getting something of their "feel." Your time will be well spent. And remember our advice about saving your sketches; you never know when an idea which you have jotted down with the utmost abandon may be the exact thing needed as the basis of some later painting. And, if you wish, experiment also with some of these methods of enlarging.

# Chapter 18

# THIS THING
# CALLED PERSPECTIVE

MANY OF US, particularly in the case of paintings of land and sea, prefer those which lead the eye into space, exhibiting effects of depth and distance —those which possess, in other words, a three-dimensional quality created by the artist on his flat, two-dimensional canvas. We like the eye to be led into the picture by degrees from foreground to middle distance, with at least glimpses of distance—perhaps extreme distance.

One of the most amazing, and appreciated, abilities of the artist is this skill of his, when arranging his compositions, to create on his absolutely flat canvas surface this illusion of depth and space.

How does he do it? How can *you* obtain such effects? Briefly, by coming to understand through observation, study and firsthand practice, the laws behind nature's appearances as seen by the eye of man. Among these are the laws of perspective.

### PERSPECTIVE CONVERGENCE

Doubtless the obvious pictorial way to lead the eye into space is the familiar one of converging receding lines perspectively to, or towards, one or more distant "vanishing points." This is a matter of drawing, rather than of painting. Sometimes the converging lines meet at a single van-

*Figure 52*
**PARALLEL PERSPECTIVE**
*Through such perspective
we can lead the eye
into space, creating a
third dimension.*

ishing point within the picture area, and at the level of the eye (horizon), as in Figure 52. This type of perspective is called "parallel" or "one point." Again, the lines converge towards two or more vanishing points, often outside the canvas but still at eye level, as in Figure 53. (With the leading

*Figure 53*
**ANGULAR PERSPECTIVE**
*Here the building, turned
at an angle, again has a
three-dimensional quality.*

objects thus turned at an angle, this type of perspective is termed "angular.") Some receding lines which are not horizontal in the objects depicted (but which slant up or down) will converge to points well above or below the eye. See Figure 54. Each series of receding parallel lines converged to its own vanishing point; we therefore have as many vanishing points (on or off the canvas) as there are series of receding parallel lines.

In other words, *all receding lines which, in the objects depicted, are actually parallel one to another, appear to converge towards the same point.* If converging parallel lines are horizontal, they will seem to meet at a vanishing point at the eye level (horizon).

*176*

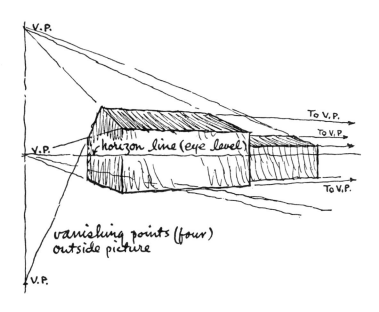

*Figure 54*
**OBLIQUE PERSPECTIVE**
*When vanishing points are above or below the eye, we refer to the perspective as "oblique."*

The perspective line arbitrarily called the horizon is always at the level of the spectator's (painter's) own eye. If you stand above your subject matter—on a hilltop, for example—the horizon line in your drawing or painting will be very high, as in Figure 55, A, giving the impression of looking down on your subject; you develop what is known as a "bird's-eye (airplane) view." The higher your position in relation to your subject, the higher the horizon line will be, for remember it is at your own eye level. If a subject is above the eye, so that you are looking up at it, the horizon will be low in relation to it (still at your own eye level). You create an effect sometimes described as a "worm's eye view." See 55, B.

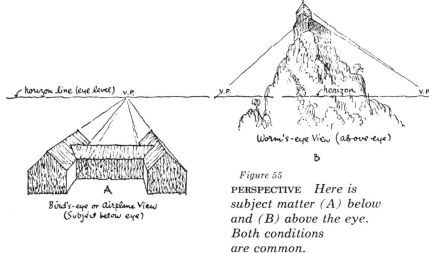

*Figure 55*
**PERSPECTIVE** *Here is subject matter (A) below and (B) above the eye. Both conditions are common.*

The closer you are to an object, the more acute these perspective appearances will be. If, for example, a building in a drawing or painting reveals acute perspective convergence and foreshortening, as at A, Figure 56, the trained observer will instantly realize that the spectator is

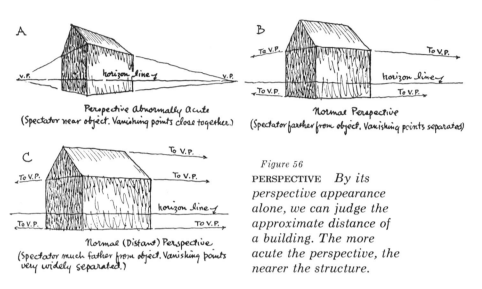

A

Perspective abnormally acute
(Spectator near object. Vanishing points close together.)

B

Normal Perspective
(Spectator farther from object. Vanishing points separated)

C

Normal (Distant) Perspective
(Spectator much farther from object. Vanishing points very widely separated.)

Figure 56

PERSPECTIVE  *By its perspective appearance alone, we can judge the approximate distance of a building. The more acute the perspective, the nearer the structure.*

assumed to be standing quite near the building; not only will the angles of convergence be sharp and all planes greatly foreshortened, but the vanishing points will be relatively close together.

One should never force an acute perspective as at A if attempting to portray a distant object. In Figure 56, B, the spectator is farther from the building, and the perspective is considerably less acute, the vanishing points being more widely separated. This gives a more normal and restful appearance. In Figure 56, C, the building is still more distant, so is drawn with its vanishing points very far apart—way outside the picture limits. (It would have been more logical in these illustrations to draw B smaller than A, and C smaller than B.) When buildings or other objects are in the extreme distance, as in C, they reveal very little evidence of perspective convergence. In short, we can usually estimate, by the way an object is drawn in perspective, whether it is meant to be near-by, in the middle distance, or far away.

Tied up with this matter of convergence—actually the cause of it— is the basic fact of perspective that *objects appear smaller in proportion to their distance from the eye.* A tree close to us appears very large; the same tree in the middle distance looks rather small; in the extreme distance it may be but a speck. Therefore, if the artist is trying to create on his canvas a feeling of space and depth, he must attempt to draw all objects at the proper size in relation to other objects according to their relative distance from the spectator. (A persistent and naive characteristic of much work by primitive painters derives from their inability to paint individual objects at the proper size, one in relation to another. Near-by objects are likely to be too small, if judged by normal standards, and distant ones too large.)

This entire subject of perspective is so complex that whole books have been written about it. We have here attempted nothing more than the briefest demonstration of the important part which linear perspective plays in creating effects of distance and space. Perspective of course serves other uses—so many that the artist with a knowledge of perspective possesses one of the greatest secrets of visual appearances, along with the power to depict his subjects convincingly. Without such knowledge, he must fumble, feeling his way, relying on "the eye." The interested reader would therefore be wise to study some of the books on perspective (*not* the complicated ones dealing with "instrumental" perspective; they are primarily for the architect and engineer), for nothing in the work of the novice reveals his lack of knowledge more quickly than does faulty perspective. One suitable book at the start is *Perspective Made Easy* by Ernest Norling (The Macmillan Company). Another—though far from new—is *Elementary Freehand Perspective* by Dora Miriam Norton (Sterling Publishing Company).

We should perhaps point out, though, that the painter, having acquired a knowledge of basic principles, seldom works by rule. *He may even defy the perspective laws if by so doing he can create the desired effect.* He may, for example, exaggerate perspective foreshortening in order to dramatize his subject matter, or he may, in the interest of better composition, place his horizon higher or lower than normal.

Possibly we should add that not all perspective has to do with straight lines. We can lead the eye into the distance by means of curved lines, as indicated in Figure 57. By receding roads, paths, walls, fences, fur-

*Figure 57*
**AERIAL PERSPECTIVE**
*Gradating color and
focus also creates the
effect of distance.*

rows of plowed ground, and a hundred other details, we can gain a three-dimensional appearance.

### AERIAL PERSPECTIVE

There is another type of perspective by which effects of distance are gained. This is known as "aerial" or "air" perspective. In this, space is expressed by means of gradations of distinctness, color, etc. If an object is near-by—clearly within our best range of focus—we see it in great detail. Take a tree close at hand, for instance. Trunks, limbs, leaves—all are clear. (We have a hint of this at A, Figure 57.) Such a tree also has a three-dimensional roundness or modeling as revealed by light and shade. If we view the tree (or a similar one) from some distance, much of the detail will disappear; it will look flatter, probably exhibiting less tonal difference between areas in light and shade. (B, Figure 57.) If viewed from a still greater distance it will be misty, vague, scarcely more than a soft silhouette. (C, Figure 57.)

There is a double cause for this: First, our vision is not well adapted to seeing distant things distinctly; second, as things become more and more distant they are veiled by the atmosphere with its mist and innumerable particles of dust. This dust and mist also affect colors, which almost never appear as bright when viewed from a distance as when close at hand. If you study a green field running far off into space, for instance, the brightest, most colorful areas will normally be those near you.

Sometimes this aerial perspective is developed in a painting by means of a series of easy stages, the eye being led gradually from the foreground to middle distance to distance, more or less as done in **Figure 57.** Again, abruptness may take the place of transition, the eye being presented with a strong contrast between powerful near-by subject matter and restrained things far away, as in Figure 58. In short, there is no rule.

*Figure 58*
CONTRAST *Distance and detachment are created by contrasting near and distant objects.*

# Chapter 19

# DEPTH, DISTANCE, DETACHMENT

LET US CONTINUE our discussion of some of the methods used by the artist who is seeking to obtain a convincingly naturalistic effect on his canvas—particularly the methods on which he relies for creating, upon his flat, two-dimensional picture surface, illusions of depth and distance—a third dimension.

We saw in the previous chapter that linear perspective offers a most effective means of thus leading the spectator's eye into space. We also learned that aerial perspective affords a second means. We hope that it is clear that these two means are usually employed in combination; not only should every portion of the subject be properly drawn in size and shape (with special reference to its perspective treatment) but its values and colors should be so adjusted throughout as to make near things seem near and more distant things at their proper distance.

### GRADATION OF TONE

Values as we see them in nature are of every kind, some of them "flat" (uniform in tone throughout) and others graded (from light to dark, from dark to light, or from one color to another). Look around you now and you will find an endless variety of tones, both flat and graded.

*181*

The artist soon learns that graded tones are particularly useful, as they provide one of his best means of gaining on canvas many of the effects which he seeks. This is true whether his purpose is to give a single object a feeling of three-dimensional form, or whether he wishes to create in a larger way a sense of space or distance. Gradations of tone are useful, too, in obtaining impressions of separation or detachment of one object from another.

### MODELING THROUGH GRADATION

To exemplify the use of graded tones in creating a three-dimensional character in a single object, let us consider the sphere. At 1, Figure 59, a

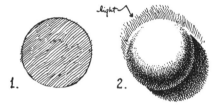

1.

2.

*As the effect is flat, this might be either a disk or a sphere.*

*Through gradation, a third dimension has been indicated.*

*Figure 59*
THE SPHERE  *By grading tones, you can transform a flat disc into a sphere.*

uniform flat tone has been used. Here we are aware that the object is round, but we have no way of judging whether its surface is flat, concave or convex. Only by using graded tones (as at 2) to represent variations of light and shade, can we so model this form as to give a satisfactory three-dimensional impression.

This sphere is typical of most rounded objects; some gradation of tone is almost essential if we are to express their third dimension.

Unlike the sphere, flat-sided solids such as the cube (which is typical of many) can often be rendered satisfactorily by means of flat tones, as at 1, Figure 60. What is not so commonly realized is that such flat-

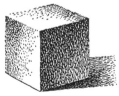

1 · Flat tones    2. Graded tones

*Figure 60*
THE CUBE  *Graded tones offer advantages with both rounded and flat forms.*

*Figure 61*
GRADATION  *Here dark
tones grade back to
a light center.*

sided objects can also be well expressed through the judicious employment of graded tones. Every tone at 2, for instance, is graded. (We use the word "judicious" advisedly, for it must be admitted that graded tones, when utilized for the expression of plane surfaces such as those of the cube, can all too easily create warped or twisted effects. Therefore they must be handled with care. Those at 2 have purposely been exaggerated in degree of gradation in order to emphasize our point that plane surfaces can be well expressed by means of grades.)

### GRADING INTO DISTANCE

Not only can gradation thus prove useful in the interpretation of individual objects having either curved or plane surfaces (including the human head), but—returning to the main theme of the present series of chapters, the composition of a painting—such gradations can be of the greatest help in leading the eye wherever wanted in a composition. To exemplify this latter thought in a simple manner, we offer Figures 61 and 62. In 61, much of the subject matter—the road, for instance—has been made dark in the foreground, gradually becoming lighter and lighter as it recedes, thus leading the eye from foreground to middle distance to distance. If an entire painting were based on this procedure, the corners and edges of the canvas would be relatively dark. In Figure 62, exactly the opposite use has been made of gradations, as they run from light in the foreground to dark in the distance. A painting using this plan of composition would

*Figure 62*
GRADATION  *In this
case the gradation leads
to a dark center.*

*183*

lighten towards the corners and edges, or at least would be made indefinite there.

### GRADATION ABOUT CENTER OF INTEREST

This all ties in with what was demonstrated in Chapter 16 on creating a center of interest or focal point. Graded tones are invaluable in this connection. In Figure 63, the front of the building, together with the area im-

*Figure 63*
PLANNED GRADATION
*In this composition,
gradation is used to
promote a focal point.*

mediately around it, has been developed as the center of interest, made effective through contrasts of light and dark. The tree masses at the extreme left have been graded dark against the side of the building, which was left white in its more distant areas (A). The side of the building has in turn been graded from this white to dark at the nearest building corner (B). This expedient accentuates the apparent length of the side of the building, and throws its nearer portions into adequate contrast with both the front facade and the ground plane, the latter darkened (S) by the building's shadow. Similarly, the sky has been darkened gradually from left to right so as to create the desired contrast with both the side and front of the building. From the foreground, a light tone of shrubbery has gradually been darkened as it recedes toward the front facade, terminating in the dark, accented group of figures. In other words, through an understanding manipulation of gradations of tone, the artist of this little three-inch-wide sketch has developed a number of interesting tonal effects while forming striking contrasts about the center of interest. Often the painter finds it to his advantage thus to work for such "contrived contrasts," though he perhaps makes them less evident than in this purposely dramatized example.

*184*

In Figure 64, we again see how grades can be used to obtain effects of distance. From a light foreground, the walks and lawns (with their landscaping) grade darker as they approach the building, which is quite

*Figure 64*
**PLANNED GRADATION** *Here gradation is used to create the effect of distance.*

sharply silhouetted against the sky and distant trees. The circle of enclosing trees was purposely graded from rather dark at the edges of the composition to light as it disappears behind the building. Similar gradations are often used in painting distant mountain ranges, as in Figure 65.

*Figure 65*
**PLANNED GRADATION** *The feeling of mist is created by strong contrast.*

This is a natural treatment as so many valleys actually exhibit this effect of mist, each range of mountains growing sharp towards its ridges. (It will be remembered that the ancient Orientals were particularly skillful in using this type of gradation in their telling representations.)

The realistic painter might well ask, "But is all this true to nature?" To an extent, yes. Not only do many individual objects reveal gradations, as we have already seen in the case of the sphere, but the spectator, because of the limitations of normal eyesight, creates gradations of his own as he consecutively brings one area and then another into focus. These gradations alter in direction and degree—though he is seldom aware of it—every time he shifts the eye. Don't forget that whenever you look at an object in nature—let us say a tree or a house—for that moment it becomes your center of interest or focal point. It is here that you find—and render—the clearest details, the strongest colors, the most definite contrasts of tone. Unless you shift your eyes in other directions (which you are almost certain to do, though you theoretically shouldn't if you are working for a truly naturalistic effect), everything else will be "out of focus"—fuzzy, indefinite. The farther such areas may be from your "line of sight" or "direction of looking" and its resultant center of interest, the more blurred they will seem. Between the center of interest and these out-of-focus areas, the degree of sharpness of contrast will gradually lessen. In other words, nature's tones as seen by man will grade.

We have also learned, however, that when the artist paints from nature it is natural for him constantly to shift his eye (line of sight) and automatically adjust his focus, seeing distinctly first one area and then another. If he paints each area as he sees it when thus "in focus," his finished result may all too easily be confusing, with nothing subordinated or simplified. Too many things, all in focus, will compete for attention.

That is why the artist must learn to "contrive" or adjust his contrasts as a means of composing his subject, he will often make preliminary sketches, deciding through experience and experimentation what he will emphasize or subordinate. And in making these sketches, he will find the use of tone gradations of the utmost value.

### DETACHMENT

As you view things in nature, you have no trouble in recognizing that many of them are separated one from another. In your paintings, however, you may find that one object seems inclined to attach itself to another. A tree or a cloud, instead of going down behind a roof as it should, will seem to rest upon the roof. Some distant object may perversely insist on attaching itself to a thing near-by.

To prevent or overcome such an effect, gradations of tone may be just the thing. Compare A and B, Figure 66. In A one feels that the chimney

A

B

Lacks detachment

Graded for detachment

*Figure 66*
PLANNED GRADATION *Here gradation is used to clarify the position of an object in the composition.*

is just about as close at hand as the ridge. In B, on the contrary, there is no doubt but that the chimney goes behind the roof. This effect was created by three means: First, less and less detail was shown on the chimney in B as it approached the ridge. Second, the chimney was gradually lightened—graded down from dark to light. Third, the ridge in B was made sharper than in A so as to emphasize still further the contrast.

Such contrived contrasts should not, of course, be too evident. The spectator viewing the picture should get no feeling that it has been artificially tricked up. In the accompanying illustrations (as in other parts of the book) the pen-and-ink medium was chosen rather than oil paint as it was desired to exaggerate or dramatize each point in order to bring it emphatically to the reader's attention. In your paintings you can manage such matters with far greater subtlety. (In a painting, by the way, effects of detachment may sometimes be obtained by using one direction of brush strokes in the objects, and another in the background.)

### TRANSPARENCY OF SHADOWS

While on the matter of graded tones we might point out that one fault of many paintings by beginners—and not a few by professionals—is that their shadow tones are too black and heavy. Nature's shadows, especially those on light objects, are far from black. But sunlit areas often seem so glaringly bright that shadows, by contrast, look darker than they are. Sometimes the artist gains the shadow effect which he wants by the use of grades as indicated in Figure 67. He paints the edges of the shadow sharp and dark as at E (which makes the wall below seem brighter through contrast), grading it to a somewhat lighter tone above (F), thus gaining

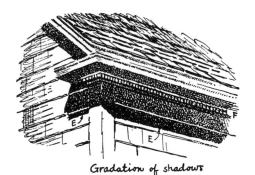

*Figure 67*
GRADATION  *By grading the tones in a shadow, you can produce the illusion of transparency. Here the edge of the shadow is dark.*

Gradation of shadows

*Ogden M. Pleissner:* HAYSTACKS AT RAILROAD RANCH
*The modeling of the dark and light planes gives a tremendous
sense of volume. Note how the gradation in the distant
haystacks places them further away. Also notice how
the shapes of the foreground figures, though smaller, are thrust
into the foreground by the fact that they are edged with light.*

an effect of transparency. (As was done in Figure 67, he may also employ a few light and dark accents within this shadow tone to add to the transparent effect.) He may, however, reverse this grading process, as in the case of the projecting beam in Figure 68. Here the shadow is sharpest and darkest where the beam touches the wall, grading lighter and lighter below. Notice also the several graded tones on the beam itself.

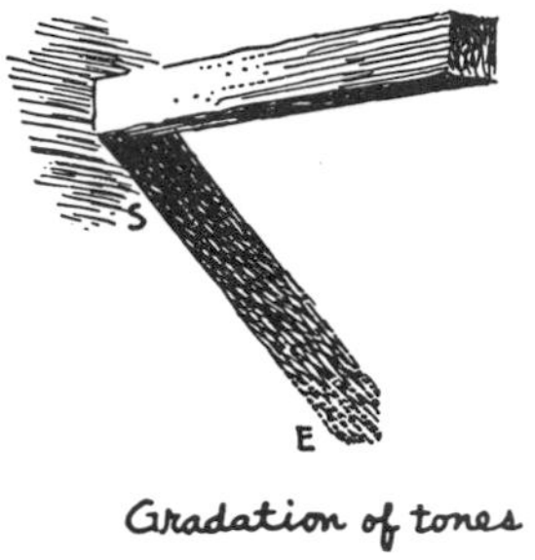

*Gradation of tones*

*Figure 68*
GRADATION *Unlike Figure 67, the edge of the shadow here is light, darkest at the center.*

### GRADED COMPOSITION

In this limited space we have been able only to hint at some of the valuable uses of graded tones. Through your own observation and experimentation you will discover for yourself how expressive such tones can be. Sometimes, in composing a painting, you may find it natural to grade the entire composition from dark above to light below (Figure 69), or vice versa. There is, however, no point in "forcing" such a condition. If it works out naturally, all right; otherwise, forget it.

As a final word on graded tones, we remind the reader that gradations are by no means confined to values of light and dark; color gradations can be even more effective, one color being graded into another. For

*Figure 69*
GRADATION *Here the entire composition grades from dark above to light below.*

189

examples of this, look both in nature and in paintings by others; then apply to your own work the things which you learn.

*Exercise 36: Depth, distance, detachment*
It won't be hard for you to plan exercises of your own designed to cover problems of the type discussed.

*Chapter 20*

## TREES, GRASS
## AND FLOWERS

ANYONE WHO STARTS to paint out-of-doors is soon confronted with a far-from-easy problem—the representation of such features as trees, bushes, grass and flowers. In a general way we have been familiar with such things all our lives, but until we face them with the intention of painting them, most of us don't realize how varied, how complex, how utterly confusing they are. I have known more than one beginner who was ready to give up painting in disgust after a single morning in the open, bewildered by nature's superabundance of detailed subject matter. Students soon learn, however, that if they can master a few comparatively simple fundamentals their troubles will largely vanish. A lot depends on developing the right approach.

As to trees, let me repeat an earlier word of advice: when you set forth on your first tree-painting expedition, don't select specimens which are near-by. If you do, you will see a multitude of leaves and branches of all sizes and shapes, possessing every minor variation of light and shade and many a nuance of color. Even if, instead of a tangle of inter-twined trees such as you so often find, you choose a single near-by specimen, you are scarcely better off, for it will loom over you, a terrifying giant. How can you possibly shrink this thing to fit the modest limits of your

*191*

canvas? Probably you can't if you sit close to it. But if you will back away from the tree—will view it from a hundred yards or more (perhaps even a quarter of a mile)—you will have gone a long way towards solving your problem. You will now see the larger masses of light, dark and color rather than the smaller ones. You will discover that a typical tree is, in basic mass, not unlike a sphere, an ovoid or a cone (Figure 22). Even the more complex types of trees usually show a relationship to such geometric solids, though sometimes each will suggest a group of such solids, rather than a single solid (Figure 22, B). As you draw or paint a tree, keep this in mind. But don't get the notion that tree contours are necessarily rounded, for they are not. Often, in fact, trees can be bounded with lines for the most part straight—see Figure 70.

Straight boundaries

*Figure 70*
TREES *The main contours of trees can usually (though not always) be largely bounded by straight lines.*

### SILHOUETTES

It is true, of course, that each species of tree has its own individual characteristics. Often it has a distinctive shape by which it can be identified at a glance, no matter how distant it may be. By way of preliminary study, it would be a good idea for you to try representing a few trees in silhouette

*Figure 71*
TREE SILHOUETTES *Trees can often be recognized by silhouette alone.*

alone, more or less as was done in our little ink silhouettes, Figure 71. (Use ink if you wish.) This should impress upon you the importance of always looking for such a silhouette.

192

Yet a tree is not, of course, a flat plane against the sky, and, unless viewed at night or in the extreme distance, seldom gives that appearance. (Some evergreens may prove an exception.) Instead it is three-dimensional. It therefore has conspicuous contrasts of light and shade, much like those of any other rounded object, though somewhat more complex. Before you start to paint a tree, therefore, look at it with this in mind. The light probably comes from above—it normally does. (See Figure 72.) It

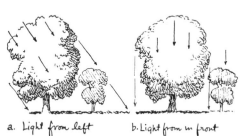

*Figure 72*

TREES *Direction of light is most important when you render trees.*

a. Light from left    b. Light from in front    c. Light from right

may slant from behind (which may emphasize its silhouette appearance). More often, however, it falls from left or right. It may fall from in front. (If a, Figure 72, were to represent the light direction in the morning, the sketch at c might represent afternoon light.)

Figure 72 demonstrates another point. Note that the distant tree looks flatter than the one near at hand. It shows less contrast of light and shade. In the extreme distance a tree often appears absolutely flat.

Though many areas of a tree may reveal minor variations of light and shade—every visible leaf, in fact, has its own variations—it is better just now to overlook such details and concentrate on the location and shape of the larger areas of light and shade, as was done in our little sketches. These shade areas are obviously the dark masses which, in contrast to the sunlit masses, give the tree its three-dimensional shape.

### PLANES

If trees confuse you because of their multiplicity of tones, it may help you to think of them as if bounded by definite flat planes, or, at least, as represented by the fewest possible tones. In the hexagonal prism at the left, Figure 73, we see that the light strikes most directly on plane a, slightly less directly on planes d and b, and quite indirectly on plane c. Try to see your trees in such simple planes. In the sketch at a, Figure 73,

*Figure 73*

TREE PLANES *Seeing trees in simple planes helps you when you are confused.*

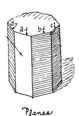

Planes    a. Two planes    b. Three planes

all areas turned somewhat toward the light are rendered as one plane and all areas turned away as another plane. At b it was decided to try a three-plane interpretation, the three planes being much like those at a, b and c in the prism sketch. The more such planes we add, the closer we get to naturalistic effects.

In many other conditions in nature it is equally helpful to attempt to see tones reduced to lowest terms, as exemplified by Figure 74, one tree,

a. Two planes plus background

b. Two planes (light against dark)

c. Three planes plus background

d. Three planes

*Figure 74*
**TREE PLANES** *You can also reduce trees to basic tones, as well as basic forms.*

or part of a tree, standing out as a flat tone against another. This is the way the poster artist frequently paints, and sometimes his results seem more expressive and satisfying than the more complicated interpretations of the painter. In other words, strive to learn the lesson of simplicity even though for the moment you take somewhat extreme means of doing so.

### SHADOWS

Trees not only exhibit light and shade but they of course cast shadows, too. These shadows may fall on the ground, as in Figures 75 and 76, c,

a. Shadows on rough grass

b. Shadows on smooth grass

c. Shadow values vary

d. Note dark shadow under bush.

*Figure 75*
**TREE SHADOWS** *Study the density and direction of shadows cast by trees.*

or on other foliage masses (Figure 76, b), or even on near-by biuldings. Bushes also have dark shadows beneath them—see d, Figure 75. The shapes of such shadows are most important; properly proportioned they

*194*

play a big part in making tree paintings convincing. Inasmuch as trees are so often made up of rounded masses, their shadows may consist of curves, too. Watch carefully the edges of tree shadows. By the irregular character of the tree shadow at a, Figure 75, we know that it is falling on rough, grassy ground, while the far more regular tree shadows at b and c indicate that they are falling on a smooth lawn and path. Note that the tree shadow on the grass is darker than on the lighter path. Tree shadows also help the artist to express the shapes or slopes of surfaces on which they fall. At c, Figure 76, the shadow indicates the pitch of the bank.

*Figure 76*

**TREE SHADOWS** *Shadows are most expressive of the forms and surfaces on which they fall.*

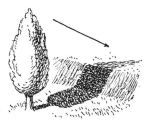

a. Foliage casts shadows on branches

b. Foliage casts shadows on other foliage.

c. Shadow shapes express the forms and textures where they fall.

Tree shadows must be right not only as to shape and value, but also in color. In this connection it is helpful to practice painting tree shadows on lawns, on ploughed ground, on roads and walks, etc.

Trunks and branches are by no means uniformly gray as beginners often paint them. Some are brownish, some grayish, some bluish. They may be green with moss or lichen. And areas which are in sunlight are *much lighter* (and often more yellow or orange) in relation to areas in shade or shadow than most students realize (see Figure 77). These

*Figure 77*

**TREE VALUES** *Trunks, limbs, and branches are by no means gray; some are very light and some very dark.*

a. Dark branches behind light branches.

b. Light branches behind dark branches.

c. Branch shadows on limbs are often seen

sketches indicate, by the way, that trunks and branches often cast shadows on other trunks and branches. Figure 76 demonstrates that

195

foliage, like branches, also casts shadows on branches and other foliage, as well as on flowers and grass. Look for all these types of shadows and represent them in your paintings.

### SKY HOLES

Foliage masses often have spaces between them through which the sky can be seen. These should preferably not be applied after the tree is finished —though often this is necessary—or they may look like highlights on the leaves. It is usually better practice to paint the entire sky first, later painting the tree over the sky. This will detach the sky, carrying it back where it belongs. To make sky holes through trees look like holes, be sure to paint the deep shade or shadow which they usually reveal, particularly along the top.

### TREE SKELETONS

Speaking again of trunks and branches, one never comes to a full understanding of trees until one has studied the shapes and plans of organization of these different "bones." Just as the student of human anatomy needs some knowledge of the skeleton of man, so the landscape artist must be reasonably familiar with the appearance of varied types of tree skeletons. In the case of dead trees, these skeletons are of course visible the year around, and so can be studied any time. Most living deciduous trees, on the other hand, reveal their skeletons completely only when the leaves are off. As to evergreens, the skeleton is often partly visible, though one must turn to dead trees for its full revelation. Figure 78 is offered as a reminder that one could beneficially make dozens of sketches

*Figure 78*
TREE SKELETONS *You don't know trees really well until you are familiar with their trunk, limb, and branch skeletons.*

of tree skeletons. Incidentally, it is usually not the perfect specimen tree which fits best into a picture but, rather, the wind-blown veteran, battle-scarred through many a fight against the elements.

Once you have learned to paint a single tree with reasonable success, you should try groups of trees, for we see most trees more or less inter-mingled with others.

As to colors for trees, don't make all your trees tiresomely green, a thing which nature sometimes does. In the early spring when trees are first putting forth their leaves, and particularly in the fall, plenty of suggestions will be found in nature for more variable color. But don't go to the opposite extreme and complicate your paintings with foliage of too many (or too conspicuous) hues.

Though, by way of simplicity, we have likened trees to spheres, in painting them it should always be kept in mind that they are living, growing things, springing from the ground—not stuck into it like balls, lollypops, or potatoes on sticks, as so many trees done by the inex-perienced seem to be.

**REFLECTIONS**

We have learned that numerous objects in nature have surfaces which are smooth and shiny, and therefore possess the power to act as mirror-like reflectors. This is the case with many leaves; just as a mirror often re-flects a bit of the sky, so can a shiny leaf. If the sky is blue, this means that the leaf will reveal an area of blue (somewhat modified, perhaps, by its own natural color). If each of a thousand leaves on a tree mirrors a bit of blue, it logically follows that the color of that portion of the tree will take on a somewhat bluish, or bluish-green, cast. Lily pads, shiny blades of grass and the smooth bark of trees are among the numerous other things which may, for this same reason, become modified in hue. So look for this bluish tone when you paint, and indicate it if it seems essential.

Leaves of trees can affect colors in another way. I remember driving through the White Mountains of New Hampshire one afternoon when the autumn foliage was in full splendor. Elms, maples and oaks arched the roadway, and a bright sun shone through their masses of yellow, orange and red leaves. Exactly as sunlight passing through a stained glass window can tint the light of a cathedral interior, so the sun penetrating the myriad leaves gave a warm glow to everything beneath. My gray car took on a light yellow-orange cast, and a white envelope from my pocket, purposely exposed to the light, showed much the same yellowish hue in even stronger intensity.

Which brings us again to the fact that if you are to picture nature well, you should learn to look for, and try to understand, the reasons behind all such appearances. In most of these things, nature herself, as you study her constantly, will prove your best teacher.

As to the actual technical handling of a tree—things like the kind and direction of your brush strokes—it is next to impossible through either the printed or spoken word to give more than a few general suggestions. Most of your knowledge will have to come as you experiment on your canvas. You can learn much, though, by studying original paintings by others as these often reveal something of the creative procedure.

As a general rule, from observation of trees in nature you will discover that the nearer leaves stand out lighter than the leaves behind them, which will often be in shadow. It is therefore frequently a good plan to first underpaint both the light and shade areas of a tree somewhat darker than they are eventually to appear. Then add your lighter paint to suggest the near-by leafy detail. The type of brushwork will depend on many things: the kind of tree, its nearness, how prominent it should be in the finished painting, etc. The finer leaves can sometimes be represented with a sort of stipple in which a single brush stroke—an old broken-down brush is often good for this—or even the dab of a bit of sponge will represent many leaves. But don't stipple everything! Dry-brush work, in which the roughness of the surface breaks the stroke, is sometimes useful in indicating not only foliage masses, but the tiny branches of trees as we see them in winter, grouped against the sky.

Whatever tool you use, you can't possibly paint each leaf, so your job is to indicate—to create a satisfactory illusion. And so it is when you come to bushes, grass, and masses of flowers. Ultimately, you will develop what might be called "tricks" of representation, as well as formulae for procedure, which, with some modification to suit special cases, you can utilize again and again. These tricks and formulae will play a big part in your personal painting style.

Flowers seen in beds or groups, by the way, should rarely be painted individually. Treat them broadly, *en masse*. Incidentally, the edges of a group of flowers—or of a tree or bush—are most expressive. Treat well the contours of any such mass and the rest will almost take care of itself.

One more point: In rendering leaves, grass and flowers, never forget that they are, in comparison with much outdoor subject matter, soft and yielding, and capable of motion. Try to paint them that way!

*Exercise 37: Trees and foliage*
This whole chapter is full of suggestions for your guidance, so what more need we say? We might mention just one last thing: Collect good photographs of trees for reference.

# Chapter 21

## STONES AND
## STONY FORMATIONS

UNLIKE FOLIAGE, discussed in our last chapter, rocks are hard, unyielding and heavy. Something of these characteristics should be caught in one's pictorial interpretation. I was about to add that rocks are dull and gray, but this is only relatively so. While they seldom have hues as brilliant or varied as those of flowers or foliage—particularly autumn foliage—they are by no means neutral. Many are to some degree red, orange, or brown, and as many more show indications of blue, violet, and even green. In other words, you can't properly paint all rocks with mixtures of black and white or with any one single hue.

On the whole, beginners paint rocks too dark and too gray. Actually, rocks often appear practically white, or a bit yellowish from the sun. (I am thinking not only of white or off-white rocks—certain marbles, lime-stones, etc.—but of many species as we see them exposed to bright sun-shine.) Again, if stones are smooth, their lighted surfaces may take on a bluish cast resulting from the fact that they mirror to at least a slight degree the blue of the sky. Other stones are green with moss, gray with lichen, or brown from attached particles of earth.

### WHAT ARE ROCKS?

Perhaps I should interrupt to explain that by "rocks" I am thinking not only of individual specimens but also of collections or groupings as we find them in river beds, at the base of landslides, etc. And I particularly have in mind such large stony formations as we see in mountain tops, rocky cliffs or headlands, ledges or outcroppings—things which play an important part in many a landscape or marine painting.

Such formations vary amazingly not only in color but in shape and physical makeup. While they are less troublesome to the artist than foliage, it is not easy to represent them convincingly. Yet careful examination usually reveals some indication of the natural laws which created or arranged them. Often, for instance, we find our rocks disposed in horizontal strata—layer on layer of almost continuous bands. (See Figure 79, a.) Again the strata are bent or twisted, or the rocks have been heaved

*Figure 79*

ROCKY FORMATIONS *The formations of rocks often follow definite laws as to disposition and, hence, as to appearance. Individual rocks, however, are frequently jumbled into disorderly heaps.*

a. Rocks in horizontal strata

b. Sloping rock masses

c. Rounded rocks, note similarity of shape

d. Outcroppings of ledge.

on end or the strata have been tipped into a slanting position (see b). Volcanos, glaciers, streams or the ocean have thrown them about or worn them away. Many rocks are partially buried in the ground, and should be so indicated.

When you have picked a rocky subject, before you start to draw study the masses before you. See if you don't find the same shapes repeated again and again, or much the same arrangements duplicated (c). If so, this may be the key to your representation. Remember, too, that rocks are almost never seen by themselves. When not partially buried in the earth, they are surrounded by grass or leaves, or overgrown with vines (c and d).

201

The main point which I am trying to make is one which has been my constant theme—it is so important that I purposely repeat it: *If you wish to paint nature well you must get to know her well.* This involves careful examination of every detail of your subject matter, and intelligent thought as to why it looks as it does. Whether your subject is a ship or a cow, a mountain or a molehill, it is controlled by nature's universal laws governing such things as perspective, light and shade, and color. Don't forget to study all sorts of subject matter in sunlight and moonlight; observe the effect of mist, clouds, rain, hail, snow, wind. Then when it comes to any detail such as rocks, you know that there can be no rules for painting them, for you have become aware that all these things vary greatly in effect under different conditions. Yet you will realize that there are universal laws which caused all their varied appearances and will help you to understand them.

It's not a bad thing, as I've said before, to concentrate now and then on some one kind of subject matter. If rocks are your subject at the moment, take long walks, sketchbook in hand, comparing the types along the way. Study good photographs, too; they will show you many types not found in your vicinity. You will discover some to be sharp—perhaps slaty—with correspondingly crisp contrasts of value. Others are soft and crumbly, and therefore possibly rounded in contour. Some are full of cracks. As to texture, some are rough and some smooth.

*Exercise 38: Rocks*

Utilize as many as you can of the above suggestions, and such others as occur to you. Because of such variations of form and hue as we have demonstrated, the artist has considerable leeway when using rocky formations in his compositions. He can make them large or small, smooth or rough, light or dark, and of practically any color. But when he's through, they must look like rocks!

# Chapter 22

# WATER AND
# REFLECTIONS

IF ROCKS OFFER PROBLEMS, water can prove far more troublesome. Even calm water, with its reflections, can give the artist many trying hours, and when he is confronted with the ever-changing effects of ripples, waves, rapids, and waterfalls, some of them accompanied by foam and spray, he has challenge enough to keep him busy for many a painting session. Rain, too, is a thing to think about. It not only tends to soften or obscure much subject matter, dulling nature's tones, but when rain falls on a street, a sidewalk or a building roof, it instantly converts it into a series of huge mirrors, complicated with reflections.

Speaking of rain, many landscapists, especially those favoring such huge spectacular subjects as were portrayed by the Hudson River School, have shown in the background an approaching shower, or perhaps a rainbow against dark clouds.

Haze, fog, and mist are other forms of water—forms which, as we have seen, greatly affect many of nature's appearances. Snow and hail, too, are but frozen rain. Hail seldom affects the artist, but I don't need to point out how snow alters the appearance of all outdoors.

### CALM WATER

This is the easiest to do. Your main job is to make sure that the water as you paint it looks flat, not tipped up. Horizontal strokes will usually

*Figure 80*
**WATER AND REFLECTIONS**
*Brush stroke directions
vary with different
types of reflection.*

a. Horizontal strokes for water   b. Vertical strokes for water   c. Free strokes

do the trick (Figure 80, a), though when water mirrors fairly definite images, vertical strokes may help you to express them (b). In this latter case, a few horizontal strokes sometimes heighten the effect, as in this sketch at b. Reflections, by the way, are usually, though not always, darker than the subject matter reflected. If calm water shows clear reflections, much as a mirror would do, a big part of the artist's job is to see that they are correctly drawn. (Figure 81, a.) Only one versed in perspective or possessing the rare natural skill to portray such things convincingly, can quickly and accurately draw reflected forms. (You can get some help by experimenting with a mirror, laid flat. Put small objects on this mirror and sketch both objects and reflections.)

### SHADOWS ON WATER

To complicate effects still further, the sun often casts shadows on water. These shadows are especially noticeable when the water is calm. If, for instance, a rowboat is on the water, we can see not only the inverted reflection of the boat but also, riding the surface of the water—it may be very faint—the shadow of the boat as cast by the sun. When water is muddy, this shadow sometimes becomes quite distinct.

Water in sunshine, incidentally, often throws shimmering light upward to illuminate the under side of the hulls of ships, of projecting wharves—of anything, in fact, which is there to receive it.

### WATER IN MOTION

Even the calmest millpond (Figure 81, a), with its clean-cut reflections, is seldom at rest for long. A bit of breeze springs up, or an oarsman

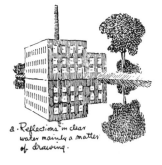

*Figure 81*
**WATER AND REFLECTIONS**
*Whether water is smooth
or rough, it picks up
colors by reflection.*

a. Reflections in clear water mainly a matter of drawing.   b. Reflections break up as water gets rougher.   c. Rough water is still a reflector

# Chapter 23

## SKIES AND CLOUDS

LIKE MANY of the other details discussed in recent chapters, skies and clouds are so important that entire books might well be written concerning them. As a matter of fact, Eric Sloane *has* written a book, entitled *Clouds, Air and Wind* (Devin-Adair), which introduces us to the different types of cloud formations, and the altitudes at which they might be found. It would pay you to study this book.

### ADJUSTMENTS

Yet the landscape artist, no matter how much he may learn about skies and clouds, often takes liberties with them, employing them according to his purpose. In this respect, skies and clouds give the artist unusual freedom; they are, in fact, one of the few things in nature which he can manipulate almost at will. He may, for example, decide to use a large

a. Clouds here constitute
the dominant motif

b. The sky is adjusted to
complement the subject

c. Dramatic sky contrasts
are often created.

**Figure 82**
SKIES AND CLOUDS  *The artist utilizes skies and clouds almost at will to create values and hue contrasts.*

sky area, as in Figure 82, a, in which a studied arrangement of clouds will be a feature of his composition. On the contrary, he may prefer to eliminate, or nearly eliminate, sky areas. Possibly he will feel that cumulus or cumulo-nimbus cloud formations (rounded at the top) will best serve his compositional purpose (Figure 82, a), while, again, he may prefer the horizontal lines of most stratus (straight) formations. Perhaps he is painting a group of evergreen trees, or a cathedral with spires, dark in silhouette against the sky. By way of contrast, he may deliberately keep his sky light, though he may darken it at the corners of his painting in order to accentuate further the silhouette through contrast. (See Figure 82, b.) A reverse plan might be followed in the case of a sunlit monument or skyscraper. This might well be set off against a very dark sky (Figure 82, c). If a building is dark in some areas and light in others, the artist, in rendering his sky, may reverse these values so that, in final effect, light sky will be contrasted with the dark building areas and dark sky with the light (Figure 83, a). Similarly, in painting mountains, a dark sky may be utilized behind a sunlit peak, while a light sky or clouds will give the desired contrast behind the shaded mountain areas (see 83, b).

a: A "contrived" scheme of values, with
contrasts developed throughout.

**Figure 83**
SKIES AND CLOUDS
*Further ways in which the artist contrives the desired contrasts.*

b. Another contrived scheme, with values
dark against light and light against dark.

These contrived contrasts will by no means be confined to values alone. He will also exercise similar color control. The colors used for the rest of his subject matter will often influence him in his choice of colors for a sky. He may work out an analogous color scheme, or one of strong contrasts. He has quite a range of hues at his command, for "sky blue" can run a long gamut from greenish-blue to purplish tones. In addition, we know that skies often exhibit a wide variety of warm tones, including the brilliant red, orange and yellow of sunrise and sunset. Of all this range, he chooses the hues which suit his purpose.

The artist's control of skies has still another application. Sometimes he is interpreting in a painting a quiet, peaceful mood, and so he renders his sky simply and unobtrusively. Again, he seeks a mood of liveliness and excitement, and therefore makes his sky dramatic with huge, wind-blown cloud forms, strong contrasts of light and dark, or a display of vivid hues.

In short, skies and clouds are slaves of the experienced painter who does with them more or less as he pleases, provided his final effect is consistent in appearance.

### FIELD TRIPS

Obviously, he cannot thus knead clouds to his own purposes until he knows them well. To get to know them well he must study them at first hand. This he may do through cloud-hunting expeditions. On days when nature inspires him with her cloud displays he concentrates on sketching them, perhaps in pencil, charcoal or pastel or, more likely, in watercolors or oils. This is no easy task, for clouds, like the waves of the sea, don't stand still for long, and their shapes are constantly altering. Frequently, clouds wholly melt away before one's very eyes, dissipated by evaporation.

### SOURCE MATERIAL

In this cloud-hunting work, the camera, fitted with proper filters, can come into play as a supplementary means of recording intriguing cloud forms to be used in later paintings. Many artists, too, collect pictorial magazine scrap as a further source of appropriate cloud shapes. (Seldom in their paintings do they "crib" this sort of thing straight, but, rather, they adapt it to their requirements.)

Such source material is especially useful when making studio paintings based on outdoor work. Clouds may be adapted from one piece of scrap, and an exciting tree from another, substituted, perhaps, for a more commonplace tree previously sketched at the site. And so an entire painting can gradually be developed by adaption or substitution, detail by detail. (Don't forget that in combining all such details the light must fall from one direction!)

### PROCEDURE

When you try your own first landscape work out-of-doors, you may be fortunate if the day is cloudless, or practically so. There will be enough to confuse you without the additional problems which result from having your subject alternately in sunshine and shadow. So for a while, at least, it might be well to make an effort to pick bright, clear days for your painting.

Assuming the day to be clear, you may want to follow the common practice of painting the sky first, once your subject has been sketched on your canvas. Not all artists prefer this procedure, however. Some choose to complete much of the rest of their painting first, then adjusting the sky to the previous work. Both methods have their advantages. Perhaps the best method is to develop the sky gradually as the work advances.

Skies in nature are very luminous, the light often fairly dazzling. You can't possibly get this full brilliance, but don't let it worry you too much: with luck, you can obtain an approximation.

Don't paint your sky as though it were a vertical curtain, like a theatre backdrop. We see a sky as though we were inside a huge dome. Keep this always in mind. In the distance, the individual clouds, if visible as such, will appear to be very small. Often they will merge into hazy formations. If so, paint them that way. As you look higher and higher in the dome of the heavens, the larger and more distinct the cloud shapes will commonly be.

Not only will we often discover this increase in size and this sharpening of shape as we swing the eye from horizon to zenith, but colors, too, will alter. On a bright day, the purest, most intense blue will normally be found directly overhead. From this point the color will usually lighten and soften as we folllow it down the curve of the dome until, near the horizon, it often becomes a scintillating sort of yellow-green. This transition is so gradual that you may be scarcely aware of it, but you can prove it for yourself by the simple expedient of tearing two small holes several inches apart through a sheet of white paper, then holding the paper so that you can peek simultaneously through both holes at a bit of the zenith color and another bit of the near-horizon color.

As to technical handling, the portions of the sky near the horizon can well be done with a wide brush or the blade of your palette or painting knife. Thinning your paint slightly with turpentine at this point will have a triple advantage. It will give your sky a more distant quality, will prevent the formation of disturbing ridges of paint, and will provide a quick-drying tone over which you can immediately paint trees, etc., with no trouble. Don't, if you want a convincing effect, build up roughly textured paint in those horizon areas. As you work towards the zenith, however, you may be able to use, on the nearer clouds or sky areas, somewhat more vigorous handling.

Many cloud masses—the common cumulus kind and the more dramatic thunderhead (cumulo-nimbus), for example—are somewhat spherical in general shape, or, strictly speaking, are composed of intermingled parts of spheres. (Figure 82, a.) Their light and shade are disposed accordingly. When the sun is high, they are lightest at, or near, the top, shading darker and darker at the bottom. In the case of the rain-laden thunderhead, the base is often very dark. (Occasionally, the base of a cloud—or group of clouds—will receive light reflected from other cloud masses, beneath, or from vast stretches of sunlit water, sand or fields of growing grain. Hence the tone at the base will be somewhat modified, and should be painted accordingly.) Some clouds, with their great variation of light, shade and shadow, call for an amazing amount of modeling.

As to direction of brushwork in painting clouds, there is no set rule, but horizontal stratus clouds can often be effectively handled by means of generally horizontal strokes, while the rounded cumulus types can well be rendered with curved strokes. I have known artists, though, to build up all sky areas with strokes in many directions, arguing that they thus gain a better effect of atmospheric vibration. Cloud edges are not easy to manage. Sometimes they are sharp and clean-cut against the blue of the sky (as in the case of the sunlit top of a thunderhead), while again they are extremely soft, merging by imperceptible degrees with the blue. Edges often are so complex in shape that they must be simplified.

### SHADE AND SHADOW

The shade sides of clouds vary in color under different conditions. Some are blue, bluish-gray, or gray; again warmer colors are present. Usually, in fact, cloud colors exhibit warmth.

Clouds cast shadows not only on one another, but also on the ground. A very common trick in landscape painting—especially in large works like those of the Hudson River School—is to suppress certain areas by throwing them into cloud shadow, allowing the sun to spotlight other areas. By carefully shaping such cloud shadows, the artist is able to express the surfaces on which they fall. The edges of cloud shadows are usually extremely soft in effect, never sharp—study them in nature to learn their true appearance.

### SEA AND SKY

In painting marine subjects where large areas of both sea and sky appear, there must be a close relationship of both value and hue. If the sky is very light or very dark, the water will often mirror something of these same values. (In many instances the water will, however, look darker than the sky.) If the sky is deep blue, or bluish-green, or a bit towards purple, again the water is almost certain to pick up these colors.

On a dreary, overcast day, with heavy clouds overhead, the water will also assume a heavy, threatening look (Figure 84, a). When the water is calm, definite cloud shapes, whether light or dark, are frequently reflected (b).

*Figure 84*
SKIES AND WATER  *A close relationship often exists between skies and water, as here demonstrated.*

a. The tone of the water often depends on the tone of the sky. This is also true of color.

b. Again we see how sky or clouds influence the tone of the water.

*George Elmer Browne:* PERCÉ ROCK AT GASPÉ *Here you
can see a good example of cumulous cloud masses,
boldly brushed in. Note how the brushwork suggests the
direction in which the clouds are moving, a technique which
also reinforces the thrust of the over-all composition.*

You can't hope that every painting day will be cloudless, and you wouldn't want it that way. Sooner or later you will find yourself faced with rapid cloud changes; these will cause corresponding changes in the entire landscape. Perhaps for a time the sky will be cloudless. Later, fluffy cumulus clouds may appear, only to give way, still later, to nimbo-stratus or cumulo-nimbus formations, accompanied, perhaps, by a shower. You can't hope to adjust your painting to all of these changes. Instead, you will decide which of the many effects in nature's repertoire you like best, and will finish your painting accordingly.

*Exercise 40: Skies and clouds*

Based on the above text, you should have no trouble in assigning yourself a variety of problems covering the different points touched upon and others which occur to you. Get into the hills or mountains for some of this work, if you can, for there you feel close to the sky, and are able to see distinctly many of its myriad manifestations.

# Chapter 24

# REPRESENTING BUILDINGS

IF WE CHECK all the paintings at a typical exhibition we find that buildings of one kind or another are favorite subjects. Some street scene paintings or other urban views very naturally consist almost entirely of buildings, and in many landscapes buildings either comprise the most important part of the subject matter or are used as vital accessories. In numerous shore scenes and seascapes, we discover that old fishing shacks, light-houses and fishermen's cottages run a close second to (if not ahead of) the various types of sailing craft in their marine settings.

While trim, up-to-date structures—cathedrals and skyscrapers, for instance—are among the buildings commonly portrayed, still more popu-lar, perhaps, are structures which might be described as quaint or di-lapidated—old barns, covered bridges, boat landings, windmills, etc. In recent years there has been a great run on the old mansions of the Vic-torian era, with their numerous turrets, dormers and porches, all over-adorned with the product of jigsaw and turning lathe. Often their en-vironment has become rundown; they are pictured in the midst of weedy, ill-kept surroundings—perhaps beside a railroad yard, or a modern filling station.

I am not arguing for or against any one of these types of subject, though, as a Maine native, I confess to a personal preference (in my own

*Jack Bookbinder:* ROOFTOPS, CITY HALL, PHILADELPHIA
*This architectural view is both an exercise in perspective and in
the rendering of geometric form. Note how clearly the
direction of light is defined and how this defines
the planes of the very deep shadows, an effect which
promotes a somber mood. Also notice how little detail
is needed to convey the texture of the buildings.*

work) for shore scenes, with their fishing craft, smoke houses, lobster shacks and the like.

If one is to paint buildings at all well, whatever their kind, one must know something of their structure—how they go together and how they function. I don't see how a painter can hope to paint successfully any type of building (or boat, wagon, fence or other man-made object for that matter) until he has looked it over, thought about it, and sketched it repeatedly. Even if a barn roof has caved in, or a dory has descended to doing duty as a flower box, some skill is still needed if the subject is to be convincingly portrayed.

### YOUR SKETCHBOOK

So my advice to you, if you are interested in such things, is to keep a sketchbook constantly with you, and to use it whenever you find opportunity.

Boats and ships, with their curves and complicated foreshortening, are particularly difficult to draw. A few rules of perspective can be of help, but nothing can take the place of hour upon hour with pencil and sketchbook. Buildings are just about as demanding. They have complicated steps, chimneys, roofs, dormers, and all sorts of like details which call for reasonable correctness of delineation.

Yet there is one ray of sunshine; let me again remind you that once you can draw fairly well a few geometric solids—the cube, square prism, triangular prism, hexagonal prism, pyramid, sphere, ovoid, cone, and cylinder—you are on your way to the representation of any subject matter, for remember that everything is based on one or another of these forms, or on two or more of them in combination. A barn, for example, is a square or rectangular prism on its side, with a triangular prism forming the gables and roof. A silo is often a cylinder with a flat conical top. A dome is but a hemisphere, perhaps raised onto a cylindrical drum. A barrel is a slightly swollen cylinder. A wheel is basically like the end of a cylinder.

Therefore, if you have trouble drawing such subject matter as we mention above, practice for a few evenings the sketching of these simple basic forms. You'll never be sorry. But don't limit yourself to their delineation in outline. Add their shade and shadow. Draw them outdoors in sunshine (where you see clean-cut shadow shapes) and indoors in more subdued light (where shadow edges are soft and variable).

*217*

Assuming that you already have the skill to draw your boats or buildings fairly well, what tips can be offered for painting them? Frankly, very few. As to direction of brush strokes, we have made clear that often they can follow the forms. In other words, let strokes take the direction which most naturally express the surfaces. As to surface character, let common sense be your guide. If a thing is smooth and glossy—window glass, for instance—quick, crisp strokes are often the solution. If a surface is rough, it can be scraped, overpainted when half-dry, gone over with a worn brush, stippled with the end of a brush, or otherwise manipulated until it looks right.

## BUILDING MATERIALS

I sincerely advise you to concentrate for a while on the indication of all of the common building materials as they appear in different structures and under varying lighting conditions. Paint brickwork, stonework, stucco, shingles, thatch. Here we have the same old story: you will see too much —too many bricks, too many shingles. So work for general, rather than detailed, effects. Figure 85, a, makes clear that it is by no means necessary to paint every brick or stone in a wall; suggest a few and the rest will take care of themselves.

*a. Stone details*    *b. Shadows*

*Figure 85*
BUILDING DETAILS *There are many little tricks of indication which the artist gradually acquires.*

## SHADOWS

The shadows on buildings, or cast by buildings, are very important. As they vary in shape with every shift of the sun, it is well to tie down their proportions while the sun is in one position and then leave these shapes alone. In other words, don't alter shadow forms as the sun goes on to new positions unless you feel that your painting will be much improved by the change. Many building details can be quite fully expressed by shadows alone, or by shadows plus a minimum of supplementary tone. See, for instance, the sketch offered as Figure 85, b. It's a good exercise to see if you can find a subject which you can express almost entirely in two values as was done here—white (or very light gray) for the sunshine, black (or dark gray) for the shadow. A common tendency, by the way, is to make shadows too dark in value. Try to guard against this.

*Exercise 41: Buildings*
As with previous kinds of subject matter, your course is clear. As time goes on, experiment with the representation of buildings of many types, built of different materials, and as seen at varying distances under diverse lighting conditions.

# Chapter 25

## LESSONS FROM
## MASTER PAINTERS

THROUGHOUT THIS BOOK I have repeatedly urged you to study original paintings by competent artists whenever you find an opportunity. Occasionally some artist offers contrary advice; he argues that the only way in which he can develop his own individuality, and so "express himself" in his work, is to refrain from becoming "contaminated" through exposure to the paintings of others. Surely such an artist belongs to a very small minority. I am certain that most of us agree that, as in any other field, we would be foolish, indeed, not to profit all that we can from both the procedures and finished works of master painters, past and present.

### MUSEUMS AND REPRODUCTIONS

Take advantage of the opportunities offered by the museums and libraries in your town. The master painters can all help you improve your modeling, your glazing or scumbling techniques. They can help you with aerial perspective, color harmonies, or any of the things I've discussed in this book.

The original paintings are ideal, of course. You can stand close to the canvas to study brushwork, underpainting, and other techniques which require detailed analysis. You can also stand far back and study the composition, the over-all color relationships, and so forth.

But reproductions should not be ignored either. Art books can combine collections from all the great museums in the world. In one afternoon you can thumb through renowned masterpieces. With the advances in the printing industry, reproductions are now capable of showing great fidelity to the originals.

### A WORD OF CAUTION

If any warning is needed it is merely one already given: don't make the mistake of studying, copying or imitating the work of any particular artist, no matter how much you may admire it. After all, it is *his* work, not yours, and it's far better to try to develop your own talents along natural lines and fall short of your goal than to produce work of even higher quality if it is purely imitative. In other words, in the long run there is far more honor and satisfaction in being a mediocre originator than a better imitator. But don't hesitate to borrow a good idea here and another there, adapting each to your own needs; gradually all such ideas will amalgamate to become a part of you and your own painting style. And this style will very naturally change from time to time as you develop.

### IT'S NOT OLD FASHIONED

Some seem to think it "old hat" to turn to the famous masters of the past for inspiration and help, but don't forget that in many respects the outstanding men of long ago developed the art of painting in certain directions to a point seldom if ever equalled since. But study the outstanding men of today, too. They are also making vital contributions.

Through studying a variety of subject matter and handling by artists of somewhat divergent points of view you will lay the best possible foundation on which to build your own painting career. In all this, the best of luck!

*As interviewed by* ERNEST W. WATSON, *Editor Emeritus, American Artist.*

*Reprinted with Permission*

# JOHN FOLINSBEE
# PAINTS A
# LANDSCAPE

IT HAS BECOME fashionable in some circles to turn up the sophisticated nose at painting that concedes anything whatsoever to the average person's love of beauty as seen in nature by the layman's eye. The thing to do, they say, is to look within to explore the chambers of the imagination. How empty these chambers so often are or how incoherent and boring the stuff stored therein is constantly being demonstrated in canvases that frequently surprise many of us by winning the big prizes in present-day competitive shows.

To these supersophisticates a canvas like *Hazleton Brickyard* is regarded merely as a "copy" of nature, a performance, they say, that is obsolete now that the camera with its color film has made it pointless for the painter to set up his easel outdoors.

We sent our photographer on a two-hundred-mile drive to get a picture of Folinsbee's subject so that readers could see for themselves how close a copy of the object *Hazleton Brickyard* really is. The photographer had quite a time finding it and identifying it by the photograph of the completed canvas which was all he had for a guide.

In this canvas and the demonstration of its growth and development, we see how a creative painter gets his theme from nature, then plays upon the theme with imagination and with skills acquired through long experience with the language of art.

*225*

*The old structure in the photograph is the subject which
inspired Folinsbee's "Hazleton Brickyard." The artist did not
execute his painting on the spot but from Conté crayon
sketches, three of which are here reproduced.*

This canvas, therefore, is typical of the way Folinsbee uses nature. "I believe in nature," he says, "to the extent that I get my inspiration to create from nature. Art is something seen and felt; interpreted for the public through the painter's esthetic sense—plus his technical knowledge to make this understandable—so that the observer's reaction is what the painter intends. This reaction is successful when it checks with something in the observer's experience or gives leads toward new art experiences and appreciation. This to me," declares Folinsbee, "is the function of art—communication."

STEP ONE  *This sketch was made at the site as a realistic record
of the subject, although, as is seen, it is far from a factual report.
Even in this first drawing the painter had made decisions about
modifying the structure. These first sketches were about 12 x 18.*

**STEP TWO**    *This second sketch is a study to establish the abstract elements of the over-all design. Note the addition of the two upright poles needed to create a balanced design. Here also the shape of the water mass has been determined, dictated by the linear needs of the composition.*

**STEP THREE**    *The third sketch features values and clarifies the combination of statements of the first and second sketches. The elongated structure has been changed to a squarish rectangle and the details of the forms have been established. Note the figures and reflections.*

227

STEP FOUR   *This and the remaining halftones are reproduced
from photographs of the canvas taken at intervals during
its painting. Here we see substantially what was evolved in
the second Conté sketch on the previous page. The lines have
been blocked in with a French sienna. While he worked
on the canvas, Folinsbee had his preliminary drawings before him.*

STEP FIVE   *Between the preceding stage and this one,
Folinsbee brushed pure white on those areas that were to be light
in color. This insured greater brilliancy of overlaid colors. By
painting these colors into the white while wet, cracking of the
under white is avoided. No white was applied to areas which were
to be dark in the picture. The canvas at this point showed
patches of comparative warm and cool colors—blue on shed, red
on buildings, yellow here and there; then gray in the sky,
dark lines of tower and chute and dark under bridge.*

228

Now the chances are that not another painter in the country would have been inspired by this particular subject. And certainly it would impress few people as beautiful in itself. No traveler on the highway would stop his car to admire it. So it appears that even the nature painter relies greatly upon looking within; since the subject is "his" subject, his in the sense that only because of his very personal response to it is it a suitable theme for a painting at all.

Sometimes, to be sure, the appeal of a subject is obvious; it may be color alone, or line, or values. If it is any or all of these abstract qualities, the subject may be exciting to other painters as well. If mood be the chief or only provocation for the artist's response, then we should expect the subject to belong exclusively to a painter who for reasons too mysterious to comprehend is incited by it. Since mood is the dominant quality in *Hazleton Brickyard,* as in many Folinsbee landscapes, it can be assumed that mood was its inspiration.

*Hazleton Brickyard* was not painted on the spot; none of Folinsbee's finished canvases are, although he does do a lot of sketching in color outdoors by way of enhancing an already intimate acquaintance with nature. He emphasizes that he does not work from these color sketches when painting in the studio. In doing that there would be danger of copying their color. The studio painting should be creative rather than imitative.

STEP SIX   *At this point, Folinsbee began building up the gray of the sky, then put color (deep, rather bright red) on the building. He uses very little medium with his pigments; his titanium white is quite liquid as it comes from the tube. There are still areas of bare canvas.*

STEP SEVEN  *By now, attention was being paid to details,
notably the windows. The water up to this point has been given
scant attention, because its color would depend on the building.*

STEP EIGHT  *Considerably more work has now been done in
the sky and the whole tonal scheme pulled together, dramatizing
the expression with attention to form and space.*

Folinsbee's experience in painting this picture is typical of his usual procedure. Drawings made on the spot in Conté crayon on paper usually represent the only outdoor study of the subject. On some drawings he scribbles notes of color or value and indicates things to be emphasized—lightest lights, darkest darks, or the exact character of a detail. Some drawings are nothing more than line analyses of the abstract basis of the composition. When he starts work on canvas he begins with this abstract lay-in using a faint burnt sienna line. He points out the importance of solving composition, key and emotional intention of the motive before starting to paint.

Folinsbee usually paints in the *alla prima* method, which he prefers to underpainting, glazing and mixed technique. His best canvases are painted to completion within a two-day period so that the paint right up to the finish is wet enough to be workable. To delay drying overnight he puts the canvas outdoors or in an unheated room. Slight changes are often made after the canvas has dried but no repairing of large areas.

In the "wet-in-wet" method the initial stages of the painting are very important. Just how the first pigments are applied affects the quality of the color at later stages. Folinsbee sees to it that pure white goes on all areas that are to receive light colors, stroking on the white with a large brush. Renoir underpainted his colors that way and he produced very luminous colors. By painting into the white pigment while wet, there is no danger of the white cracking as it might if the white were allowed to dry. White is not used in places that are to be dark in the picture.

STEP NINE *Here the picture, approaching its final stage, shows greater emphasis on surface qualities and texture. The surface of the canvas is almost covered, the sky has had additional attention and the water, already quite well advanced in the previous stage, has been still further developed. All that remains are minor adjustments which are seen in the color reproduction.*

*Photography for this demonstration by Robert McAfee*

Folinsbee makes a practice of applying his first colors in open tones, that is, not covering the canvas completely. Other colors overpainted thus have areas of uncovered canvas to insure greater brilliance. He builds the picture from light to dark.

Says Folinsbee, "I paint a canvas from the start considering the whole surface. In the first hour I have a thin, open scrub-in. I try for a certain amount of form, modeling as I establish the scrub-in. Also color variations—as much as I can suggest without complicating the early stages. This avoids flat, pocket-like surfaces which make future spatial development difficult if not impossible."

However inventive a landscape painter may be, if he is striving for satisfying realism he has to be governed by truths of representation. These are the truths or facts of perspective. "In nature," Folinsbee points out, "lights appear to be progressively darker and warmer with the distance. Darks become lighter and cooler. Highlights on forms are comparatively cool; halftones carry the purest color; shadows are comparatively neutral; reflected light depends upon the color reflected. Such knowledge should be used in a personal manner and emphasis or exaggeration is justified if the result attains unified balance."

\*     \*     \*

JOHN F. FOLINSBEE was born in Buffalo in 1892. He studied with Jonas Lie and at the Art Students League of New York under John Carlson, Frank DuMond and Birge Harrison. He married Ruth Baldwin in 1914 and has two children—Elizabeth (Mrs. E. W. Wiggins) and Joan Baldwin (Mrs. Peter G. Cook). The Folinsbees live at New Hope, Pennsylvania, in a beautiful home right on the Delaware River. Summers have been spent in Maine and an important amount of recent work has been based upon subjects found there.

Folinsbee is the winner of many awards received throughout his very successful career. He has an excellent museum representation and has done some murals. Although he is chiefly known as a landscape painter, he has painted many portraits.

*These are the brushes Folinsbee customarily employs on fair-sized canvases.*

HAZLETON BRICKYARD  *An oil painting by John Folinsbee*

# JAMES PENNEY PAINTS AN INTERIOR

"I FEEL IT IS of utmost importance for an artist to preserve his freedom of expression," says James Penney, "even at the expense of apparent inconsistencies in his style. Each picture should be an adventure, an expression of a new experience, a fresh idea, a new challenge, a new problem to solve. He may go to some game or concert or spectacle and miss many of the obvious things other people see and hear—the plays, the score, the music, sometimes the story—but he will concentrate on purely visual things, studying the color, the patterns, the movements, the continuity of line in movement; drinking in the mood, the atmosphere, the forms, the spirit of the occasion. But it can be almost as interesting to contemplate a tree branch, or just a wall and the corner of a room as I did in the painting reproduced." Penney continues as follows:

I am deeply concerned with nature and natural phenomena in the larger sense. Basically I am probably a realist as I am searching always to create plastic symbols of my reactions to visual experience. The artist seeks to find and express some order in the fragments of the universe that lie within his comprehension—his concept of the order, the direction, the purpose of life as he knows it. If we get too far from nature and experience and feed too long on ourselves, we become repetitious and sterile and we are likely to indulge in meaningless self-expression which becomes only an empty manner and style.

I never know how I am going to paint a picture. I do not visualize the end. I let it grow from the seed of an idea. I approach each new canvas with the confidence that, if I am sufficiently enthused and feel deeply about the idea, I can marshal my forces and carry the picture through to a happy conclusion; but each move determines the next move, and the final pattern is not rigid and predetermined, but the result of a natural growth. There are many retreats and changes and anxious moments, and many canvases end up as complete failures. As Herbert Read says of Picasso: "His faith is that what he creates out of love and with passion will be found beautiful."

The artist's work (though this may sound contradictory) is a process of discovering his subject. Often it is only at the end that he discovers what he is trying to say; only at the end that the wheat is finally separated from the chaff, the gold from the ore; only then that the form emerges, clear and strong and pure, stripped of the irrelevant and forged into a thing of beauty. In the picture which is the subject of this demonstration, what started out as an arrangement of door, wall, picture, frame, coat hangers and etching press, ended up with the subject a pattern of light across the canvas. The pattern wasn't there at all actually; it only developed as seemed necessary. The forms of the objects are secondary and are revealed only through this pattern; many are eliminated and/or changed in the final painting.

Several times I have started paintings in the process of which the subject matter has changed—a still life, for instance, might end up as a landscape. The composition might not have changed appreciably, but the objects, having been abstracted to basic forms, may suggest other objects than the originals and (the subconscious coming into play) a table, a bottle, a cigar box, and an old coat may all end up as buildings, watertowers and bridges, conjured up from some half-forgotten experience of the past. I realize then that the forms and colors I started with had interested me only because they were symbols or suggestions of some past impression.

I find it difficult if I try—and why try?—to separate direct visual experience from emotional or intellectual experience. However, on occasion I can become coolly and abstractly analytical of nature. These works which are what I term "exercise" do not interest me as pictures unless there is also some emotional response. My interest is not in the cold scientific approach, the mechanical calculation, the arid purity of the nonobjective, any more than it is in the chitchat type of painting, or

**STUDIO CORNER**  *An oil painting by James Penney*
*Courtesy Kraushaar Galleries*

the sentimental, or the factual inventory type, or the neurotic theatrics of the surrealists and "magic" realists.

At my recent show the critics went from picture to picture, calling them romantic, impressionist "in the best sense of the word," abstract, postimpressionist, expressionist, and realist; all of which together, gives some clue. What they didn't call me, gives me a better idea. I was never called a surrealist, a nonobjectivist, a naturalist, an academician, a social satirist, or a primitive, or classicist, or a cubist, or a purist, or a mystic, or genre painter.

It takes years before we mature enough to know what we are really trying to do, where our interests lie. For most of our life our painting is a record of the forming of these interests, the molding of our personalities.

*This corner of Penney's studio looking through the open door toward the printing press in the next room is the subject of the painting reproduced in this demonstration.*

237

*Photography for this demonstration by Harry H. Lott*

STEP ONE  *Attracted by
the challenge of a door
opening toward him in the
center of the picture,
Penney made a quick
charcoal sketch of a corner
of his studio to get some
impression of the pictorial
idea and scale of the forms.*

STEP TWO  *The first sketch
was followed by a second,
more deliberate charcoal
sketch in which Penney
worked for a balance of
verticals and horizontals
and determined more
precisely the relationships
of shapes. The ceiling was
lowered to create a
suggestion of depth.*

*238*

STEP THREE  *The main outlines were sketched very lightly on the canvas with charcoal, then drawn with a sable brush using a mixture of burnt umber and Prussian blue. As he worked, Penney changed lines and areas, drawing lines right through forms to emphasize the main lines of movement.*

STEP FOUR  *The colors —in a mixture of oil and turpentine medium—have been applied over the still wet drawing, blending with it in places. At this stage, the canvas is completely covered, but the drawing still shows through the transparent color.*

*239*

STEP FIVE *Between this stage and the last, a number of pen sketches were made to study the design pattern. Deeper darks were added, the angle of the picture on the wall changed, and a pattern of light cut across the picture.*

STEP SIX *The color has been applied opaquely. Next the top areas were simplified and lightened, the door narrowed and the doorway widened. The values on the stool were reversed in order to tie the color and value pattern together.*

240

Only in the last seventy-five years have we again become aware of pictorial structure as compared to the imitative painting of the nineteenth century. America is developing many artists who have an excellent command of the pictorial language. Out of it all I am sure there will be some who are more than virtuosi. The period of experiment, new styles, technical fireworks, has about run its course; from now on we should look for something more profound than the cultivation of the individuality of the artist's handwriting.

\* \* \*

STEP SEVEN  *At this stage, significant new changes were made. The confusing objects in the lower left corner were eliminated completely and the ceiling beam was simplified.*

*241*

STEP EIGHT *Here, in the completed picture, we see how the all-over design motive—a light mass surrounded by enclosing dark tones—has been developed. We see this theme gradually developing at steps six and seven with the sharpening of tonal relationships and amplification of masses. Compare this final photograph with the color plate.*

JAMES PENNEY has exhibited in most of the big national shows, in group exhibitions in many museums and colleges throughout the country, and in several one-man shows in New York—most recently at the Kraushaar Galleries. His paintings are in a number of private and public collections and his murals in the post offices of Union and Palmyra, Missouri, and in Flushing High School, New York. He also did a mural panel for the Contemporary Arts Building at the New York World's Fair, 1938-39. His work has been honored by several coveted awards.

Penney, a Missourian by birth, received his B.F.A. from the University of Kansas and later studied at the Art Students League in New York. He has taught at the Munson-Proctor-Williams Institute in Utica, New York, and at Hamilton College in nearby Clinton.

He is a member of the Audubon Artists and the National Society of Mural Painters, and a life member of the Art Students League, which he has served as board member and vice-president.

242

# JERRY FARNSWORTH
## PAINTS A
## PORTRAIT

JERRY FARNSWORTH ranks high in favor with those who know and love good painting. I use the term "good painting" in its traditional connotation; the kind of painting that inherits the ideals and the technical competence of the old masters. You can hang a Farnsworth alongside a master of the Italian, Spanish or Dutch school, not to note the influence of any individual painter or school but to observe that Farnsworth creates in the same idiom as those practitioners who have brought the art of painting to its highest peak of artistic achievement. The same principles of picture construction are seen in his work, the same informed craftsmanship, the same love of paint for paint's sake. This is not to say that Farnsworth's art merely revives or perpetuates what has gone before and is in any way reactionary. He believes in tradition, but being an alive, progressive person, he paints in a way that is of his time and that is modern in the best sense. The verdict of Farnsworth's achievement rests, of course, with posterity, but contemporary opinion places him among the foremost of America's portrait and figure painters.

A good deal of contemporary painting has practically abandoned the principles of picture-making that were universal before the onslaught of the isms. It has thrown overboard all of the past, the good along with the bad, ignoring all established criteria. It has been directed pretty largely by foreign influences, many of which are the gospel of frustration.

Farnsworth is a good antidote for this sort of thing. He has not been swayed by modern European trends. He has not been tempted by the flamboyant and the spectacular. His canvases are quiet and competent, conceived and executed with good taste. His color is rich and subtle.

*243*

STEP ONE  *The figure is placed on the canvas with broad, sweeping strokes. The head is blocked in in light and shadow, with no attempt at exact drawing and with features barely indicated. The lines in the background are the remains of an old sketch.*

STEP TWO  *In the photograph above, the development of the head can be seen. First the eyes and hair are brought up.*

STEP THREE  *Here the head is brought closer to completion. The nose, mouth, and shape of the face are made clear. Shadows and half-lights are indicated and the likeness begins to be apparent.*

"Reflected lights within the shadow should be held down and not be painted nearly as light as they seem to be. A too strong reflected light will tear your shadows to pieces and confuse the eye.

"After the large areas of light and dark of the skin and hair have been well established, start to paint the forehead . . . work down the face, modeling what happens in the brows and the eye socket. Paint the skin right over where the eye will go, without as yet considering the eye itself; then the simple shadow alongside the nose. Then the muscular construction around the mouth, but still resisting the temptation of actually painting in the red of the mouth.

"Think of the nose as part of the skin of the cheeks pulled out away from the face. The nose belongs to the cheeks and should be painted as related to the areas on either side of it.

"Match the color of the iris of the eyes and paint both in at the same time. Then the dark line of the lash and the modeling of the fold of the upper lid above it. Next the whites of the eyes, noting how far below true white they are. Paint in the dark pupil and then the highlights. Some painters leave out the highlights in the eyes altogether—I often do myself. The common error is to make the highlights too big and too white.

"Try to look at the whole head while painting the mouth. If you concentrate too strongly on the mouth alone, you will make it too hard and possibly too dark. Don't forget that when you are talking to or looking at a person you look at the eyes and are only conscious of the mouth. You never stare at a person's mouth. This is where the painter has it over the camera which sees everything on the face as equally important.

"Keep the highlights in a portrait subdued. Nothing is worse than highlights flashing all over a face. A common fault is to make the highlights too chalky.

"I am a firm believer in scraping as you go along. Not once but many times. Taking off with a palette knife the superfluous paint that inevitably builds up at several stages in painting makes the surface more workable, always simplifies and more often than not improves a picture. I scrape several times during the first sitting and always before I stop painting for the day. There is nothing lost worth saving, rather one is able to build the paint where it should be heavier.

"On the second sitting, the darks are usually pretty well dried in and need to be restored to their original depth and richness. It would be useless to work on a picture in this state without first blowing on a little retouch-

STEP FOUR *By putting half-lights and highlights in their proper relationship, the likeness is greatly improved. With the head almost finished, attention is now paid to the shirt, which is quite fully modeled before the pattern is incorporated.*

STEP FIVE *The hand and the pattern and texture of the shirt are now developed. The background has been filled in, completely covering the remains of the old sketch.*

ing varnish with a mouth atomizer. Just a few light blows are enough to restore the original color and you can work into the picture immediately without waiting for it to dry."

*   *   *

JERRY FARNSWORTH was born in Dalton, Georgia, in 1895. His boyhood was spent in Georgia and New Orleans. The family moved to New York when he was sixteen. At the outbreak of World War I, Farnsworth joined the Navy and was stationed in Washington for two years, managing meanwhile to attend night classes at the Corcoran School. After the war he studied with Charles W. Hawthorne in Provincetown, Massachusetts, where he met Helen Sawyer, who became his wife.

Farnsworth has taught in the Art Students League and Grand Central School of Art. In 1942 and 1943 he was visiting professor of art at Carnegie and artist-in-residence at the University of Illinois. In 1943 he established the Farnsworth Art School at Truro on Cape Cod and later, having built a winter home at Sarasota, Florida, opened a school there.

There is scarcely a museum of importance that does not own a Farnsworth portrait or figure painting and his brushwork has frequently been commissioned for advertising projects.

STEP SIX  *The completed portrait. Compare this with the full-color reproduction on page 245. In the photograph above, the shirt pattern photographed too clearly. Note how much more suggestive the shirt appears in the color reproduction.*

*Photography for this demonstration by Seymour Fox*

# ROBERT PHILIPP
# PAINTS A
# NUDE

THE ACCOMPANYING halftone reproductions of the early stages of a painting by Robert Philipp occupied approximately three hours' work, photographs being taken at intervals during that time. In the several days following, Philipp continued his painting which is reproduced in our color plate. We concentrated upon the initial period because the early stages of a canvas are particularly revealing of the painter's method of work and because they can be more clearly shown in halftone reproduction. After the essentials have been established at the first sitting, the development of the canvas is largely a matter of subtle adjustments which would not be revealed in black-and-white reproduction.

Robert Philipp has been in the front of his contemporaries for many years. He maintains his eminent position without recourse to innovations. He has not indulged in startling experiments; his direction and his goal today are precisely what they have always been—good painting.

It is refreshing to find a painter who is still a student of the great tradition of painting in which so few contemporaries have achieved more than a modicum of proficiency. And it is fortunate that such a painter is willing to devote some of his time to teaching. (Philipp teaches at the Art Students League and the National Academy and also has a private class.)

*250*

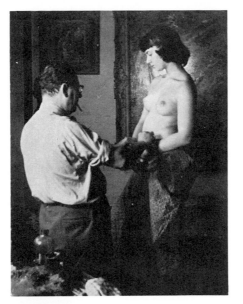

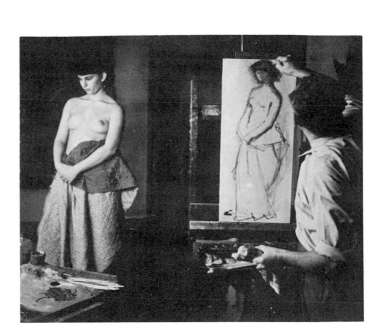

*Prior to work with his
brush, he makes a
quick sketch with a stick
of soft charcoal.*

*As an important
preliminary, Philipp
experiments with pose
and arranges drapery.*

*This is the charcoal
lay-in made during the
first thirty seconds.*

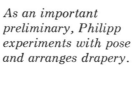

*With brownish paint diluted with turpentine, Philipp begins
with a scumbled technique, attacking the canvas with vigor.*

*This picture was taken about fifteen minutes after Philipp had begun work with his brush. The first color applied was a pinkish yellow on the breast and head; the background, cool gray above and warm gray below. The red of the drapery was also laid in.*

*During the early stages
the color throughout is
kept quite monochromatic
and very thin.*

*Occasionally he scrapes
canvas with palette knife
to prevent piling up
of pigment.*

*Stepping back from his canvas to assay results of two hours' work,
Philipp makes critical remarks about the painting's progress.*

Expert draftsmanship is implicit in good painting, and it is invariably seen in Robert Philipp's canvases. In the November 1944 issue of *American Artist* magazine this phase of his work was presented in a feature article to which readers may wish to refer in connection with the present demonstration of his painting procedure.

*On this page we see the subject gradually developing.*

*Photography for this demonstration by Von Behr*

*Portion of the painting after about two and one-half hours.*

STANDING NUDE *An oil painting by Robert Philipp*

# INDEX

258